RAMBAM

משנה תורה – יד החזקה

MISHNE TORAH

YAD HACHZAKAH

———◦(◉)◦———

A collection of Ethical and Practical Halachos

from
THE BOOK OF SEASONS II
and
THE BOOK OF WOMEN

Annotated and
Translated
by
Rabbi Avraham Yaakov Finkel

YESHIVATH BETH MOSHE
SCRANTON, PA.

Contents

———◦———

This volume of Yad Hachazaka—Mishneh Torah follows the pattern used by Rabbi Shimon Sofer in his work Musrei HaRambam which is a collection of ethical and practical halachos.

This work is not meant as a definitive guide, but rather as a description of the basic principles and ideas behind the obligations and customs of the Jewish people, as well as the ethical lessons derived from them.

Although in many places it has been pointed out that our custom differs from that mentioned in the Rambam, nonetheless one must always consult a competent halachic authority to determine the correct way to act.

YESHIVATH BETH MOSHE

הקדמה
מראש הישיבה
מורינו הרב יעקב שניידמאן שליט״א

קביעת לוח שלנו ע״פ תורה מיוחדת במה שנקבעת עפ״י מהלך
הלבנה והחמה ביחד. והיינו דבמהלך הלבנה יש חילוק חדשים
דהלבנה מתחדשת בערך כל עשרים ותשעה וחצי יום אבל ליכא
חילוק בשנה דאין ניכר במהלכו חילוק שנים ובמהלך החמה ליכא
חילוק חדשים אבל נתחלק לשנים דיש ארבע תקופות ונמצא דמי
שקובע הלוח עפ״י החמה אף שעושה חדשים של שלשים יום אינה
קביעית אמיתי של חדשים. ומי שקובע הלוח עפ״י הלבנה, חדשיהם
אין להם שייכות עם מהלך החמה אבל כשקובעים עפ״י מהלך החמה
והלבנה ביחד חדשיהם אמיתים עפ״י מהלך הלבנה וגם קביעות כל
חדש מתאים עם מהלך החמה דהחדשים נופלים בסדר התקופות
וסדר זה דרשו חז״ל מן התורה. ונראה דזה גם ביאור דרשת חז״ל
שהביא רש״י בפרשת בא - נתקשה משה על מולד הלבנה באיזו
שיעור תראה ותהיה ראויה לקדש והראה לו באצבע את הלבנה
ברקיע ואמר לו כזה ראה וקדש וצ״ב מה נתקשה למשה רבינו על
המולד. ונראה דבמצות החודש הזה לכם נכלל גם המצוה לעבר
שנים כדי שהחדשים יפלו בכל שנה עפ״י סדר שנת החמה כמבואר
בספר החינוך ובזה נתקשה דלהשוות שנת הלבנה והחמה צריך לידע
זמן המולד עד החלק בדיוק.

בהשקפה ראשונה נראה דדין לחשוב חדשים ולקדשם הוא כדי
שנוכל לקבוע המועדים בזמן השנה האמיתי אבל בראש השנה תנן
יש לי ללמוד שכל מה שעשה רבן גמליאל עשוי שנאמר אלה מועדי
יי מקראי קדש אשר תקראו אתם בין בזמנן בין שלא בזמנן ע״כ וכן
פסק הרמב״ם בפ״ב מהל׳ קדוש החדש בית דין שקדשו את החדש בין

v

שוגגין בין מוטעין בין אנוסים הרי זה מקודש ולכאורה קשה דאיך
שייך לחוג חג הראוי להיות בזמן מיוחד בזמן אחר. ומוכח מזה
דמצות קביעות חדשים ושנים עפ"י ב"ד אין החשבון כדי שנדע זמן
המועדים בעצם דאם נאמר כן אם יהיה מי שחשבונו מדוייק יותר
היה לנו לילך אחר חשבונו. אלא מוכח דהזמן הולך אחר החשבון
וכיון דניתן לב"ד הכח לחשוב ממילא שוב הולך הזמן עצמו אחר
חשבון של ב"ד.

ולבאר יותר נראה דהנה אומרים בכל יום המחדש בטובו בכל
יום תמיד מעשה בראשית וצריך להבין דאין זה מליצה אלא כך הוא
הדבר ממש והיינו דאותן השפעות שהשפיע הקב"ה במעשה
בראשית הם קיימים לעולם ובכל רגע ורגע איכא השפעה לקיים
הבריאה כמו שהיתה במעשה בראשית. מידהו צריך לידע דאף
דהשפעות דמעשה בראשית קיימים לעולם מ"מ אין העולם מתקיים
באופן שוה בכל הזמן ויש כמה אלפים השפעות שיורדים למטה ומזג
ההשפעות משתנים תמיד והעולם משתנה לפי שינוי מזג ההשפעות
והנה בכל חלק וחלק נשתנה מעט ובכל יום נשתנה הרבה. ולפי"ז יש
להבין דיסוד של זמן בכלל נתהוה מחילוק ההשפעות דכל רגע ורגע.
ונמצא אם אחד היה יודע המיזוג היה יכול לידע איזה יום בשנה הוא.
ובאמת עיקר הקובע להזמן הוא ידיעת ההשפות אלא דלפי שאין אנו
יודעים להבחין מיזוג ההשפעות אומרים הזמן כפי סדר החדשים וה־
שנים. ואף שאין אנו יודעים ההשפעה בכל עת מכ"מ במועדים נמסר
לנו בדרך כלל ענין המועד כמו שאומרים בתפלתינו זמן חרותנו או
זמן מתן תורתנו ופירושו דעיקר מה שזמן זה מיוחד אינו משום דהוא
יום טו' בניסן רק דהוא זמן חרתינו ויום טו' בניסן נתהווה ע"י השפעה
של זמן חרותנו. ועפי"ז נבין דכשקובעים ב"ד שהיום הוא עשירי
לתשרי עיקר קביעותם הוא שיש השפעות מאת הקב"ה לסליחה
ומחילה ויום עשירי בתשרי נתהוה מאותו ענין ולפי"ז נבין דהקב"ה
נתן לב"ד כח לקבוע ההשפעות שיורדים וממילא אם ב"ד קבעו שיום
זה יום עשירי נקבע כך בהבריאה דהרי מציאות הזמן הוא רק ענין
זה של חילוק השפעות. והקב"ה יסייענו להשיג ולקבל מה שנוכל
מהשפע שהקב"ה משפיע בכל עת.

SUMMARY OF
RABBI YAAKOV SCHNAIDMAN'S PROLOGUE

The Jewish calendar mandated by the Torah is unique in that it is a combination of the solar and lunar calendars. The lunar calendar, with months based on the waxing and waning of the moon, does not correspond to the solar year and seasons. Similarly, the solar calendar follows the solar seasons, but the thirty day months are arbitrary. However, the combination solar lunar calendar has real months which also correspond to the seasons.

The Sages expounded the verse "this month shall be for you the first month", saying, "Moshe had difficulty understanding when to sanctify the moon until Hashem pointed to the moon saying "when it looks like this—sanctify it.'" We can explain this difficulty as follows.

Included in the mitzvah to sanctify the new moon was the command to make leap years to intercalate the lunar year with the solar year as explained in the Sefer HaChinuch. Moshe found this difficult, because he had to know the precise amount of seconds in the lunar month, to make this calculation.

The Bais Din calculates the months and years to enable us to celebrate the holidays at the proper time. But the Mishnah in Rosh Hashanna tells us that the Bais Din's calculations are valid even if

Rabbi Yaakov Schnaidman is the Rosh Yeshivah of Yeshivath Beth Moshe Scranton, Pennsylvania.

they erred, not sanctifying the month properly. How can we celebrate the holidays on days which in fact are not holy? We see from this, that the calculation of the Bais Din is in fact what designates the actual time, thus making the day holy.

On a deeper level this can be understood as follows. Every day we say, "He who renews in His goodness each day, the work of Creation." Each day the power of creation emanates from Hashem, and just as each day differs from the day before, so too, the emanation from Hashem differs each day; in fact to a lesser degree the emanation from Hashem differs each chelek[1]. This difference in the emanation makes the passage of time. The reason one day differs from the next is because the emanation from Hashem differs. Were one able to comprehend the emanation on any given day one could know which day it was based on this knowledge alone. Although we do not comprehend the emanations of each day, we do know that on certain holidays the essence of that day is the holiness attached to that time. For example the concept of giving the Torah was manifest on the day we celebrate as Shavuos and there is an emanation for forgiveness on Yom Kippur which makes that day Yom Kippur. Understanding this concept we realize that when the Bais Din proclaims a certain day as Rosh Chodesh or Yom Kippur they are decreeing that Hashem should emanate a specific holiness at that time, making that particular day special.

Hashem should help us merit to understand and accept the holiness emanating from Hashem at all times.

---

[1] a chelek equals 3.3 seconds

TRANSLATOR'S INTRODUCTION

The previous volume contained selections from the Laws of Shabbos, Pesach, and Sukkos culled from the Rambam's *Sefer Zemanim*, Book of Seasons. This volume follows up with the remainder of *Sefer Zemanim*, namely, the mitzvah of *Kiddush Hachodesh*, "Sanctification of the New Month," and the laws of fasts, Megillah, and Chanukah. Included also are the compelling *halachos* dealing with the laws of marriage, divorce, conversion, and immoral behavior.

The mitzvah of *Kiddush Hachodesh* is the very first commandment given to the Jewish people as a whole, an indication of the overriding importance of this mitzvah. Indeed, a thousand years later in Eretz Yisrael, during the rule of the Greek-Syrian empire that reached its peak at the time of Chanukah, *Rosh Chodesh* was one of the three commandments the tyrants wanted to abolish. The other two forbidden mitzvos were Shabbos and *milah*, which shows that even our enemies ranked the observance of *Rosh Chodesh* on a plane with those fundamental commandments. For if the new month cannot be declared, there is no calendar, and without a calendar there can be no festivals, and Jewish existence disappears, God forbid.

In Talmudic times, the Sanhedrin fixed *Rosh Chodesh* on the basis of the sighting of the new moon by witnesses, and the dates were announced by messengers to the outlying regions. The Rambam describes the procedure by which the witnesses were interrogated, and we learn that the judges of the *beis din* would make accurate astronomical calculations, so that they knew when and where the moon would be sighted.

The Rambam offers a comprehensive discussion about the process by which the lunar year of 354 days is harmonized with the solar year of 365 days by introducing an extra month of Adar, which made that year a leap year. This insured that Pesach always would fall in the spring, as the Torah demands.

We learn why the the Sages instituted the second day Yom Tov to be celebrated outside Eretz Yisrael, and why Rosh Hashanah is observed for two days in Eretz Yisrael.

The Rambam gives a profoundly scientific discourse on the astronomical calculations needed for the sighting of the moon, so that a serious student would not have to resort to non-Jewish sources.

The chapters of the Laws of Fasts, Megillah, and Chanukah form the concluding sections of The Book of Seasons. We learn the little-known facts about fasts for rain, distressing circumstances, epidemics, and earthquakes.

The fourth volume of the Rambam's *Mishneh Torah* is *Sefer Nashim*, the Book of Laws Governing Relations with Women. These laws, which form the bedrock of Jewish family life are highly relevant and of crucial importance. We learn the details of *kiddushin* and *nisuin, sheva berachos*, the husband's rights and obligations, and about the mitzvah to have children. We discover the particulars of the laws of divorce and about compelling a recalcitrant husband to give a *get*. We find out about the *halachos* dealing with conversion, forbidden sexual relations, and immoral behavior. Studying the *halachos* of this section we gain an insight into many of the issues that have a direct bearing on our daily life.

In the merit of learning Torah, may we all be *zocheh* to hear, "*the sound of joy and the sound of gladness, the voice of the groom and the voice of the bride, the sound of people saying, 'Praise Hashem, Master of Legions, for Hashem is good*'" (*Yirmeyah* 33:11).

AVRAHAM YAAKOV FINKEL
Teves, 5762/2003

Mishne Torah - Yad Hachzakah

―――==◉==――

ספר זמנים
THE BOOK OF SEASONS II

Laws of the Sanctification of the New Month

Laws of Fast Days

Laws of Megillah

Laws of Chanukah

HILCHOS KIDDUSH HACHODESH

LAWS OF THE SANCTIFICATION

OF THE NEW MONTH

---◆◆◆---

THE JEWISH CALENDAR

1:1. The months of the year [referred to in the Torah and used in the Jewish calendar] are lunar months,[1] as it says, . . . *the burnt offering of the month when it is renewed*[2] (*Bamidbar* 28:14), and, *This month shall be for you the beginning of the months* (*Shemos* 12:2). To this our Sages commented: The Holy One, blessed be He, showed Moshe, in a prophetic vision, an image of the [new] moon telling him, "When you see the moon like this, sanctify it."

The years are calculated in terms of solar years,[3] as it says, *Observe the month of springtime*[4] (*Devarim* 16:1).

1:2. How much longer is the solar year than the lunar year[5]? About

---

[1]   The period during which the moon makes a complete revolution around the earth which is 29.53 days, or 29 days, 12 hours and 793/1080 parts of an hour.

[2]   "Renewal of the month" must refer to lunar months, which renew when the new moon becomes visible. Solar months are based on dividing the solar year into twelve parts which do not renew each month.

[3]   The period of time in which the earth completes one revolution around the sun which is 365 1/4 days.

[4]   Implying that Nisan must fall in the spring. To adjust the lunar calendar to the solar year, leap years must periodically be made.

[5]   The lunar year is made up of twelve lunar months.

eleven days.[6] Therefore, when [after several years] the [annual shortfall of eleven] days adds up to approximately 30 days, an additional month is added,[7] bringing the year to thirteen months. This year is called a *shanah me'uberes*, "a 'pregnant' or prolonged year."

[This must be done,] because it is impossible to have a year with twelve months and an odd number of days,[8] for it says, *of the months of the year* (*Bamidbar* 28:14). Our Sages explained: You must count months to [calculate] years, but you cannot count days to [calculate] years[9].

1:3. The moon is hidden, unable to be seen, about two days every month: roughly one day at the end of the month before its conjunction[10] with the sun, and one day after its conjunction with the sun, [before] it comes into view in the west in the evening.

The first night the moon is sighted in the west after being hidden is the beginning of the month. From that day on, twenty-nine days are counted. If the [next new] moon is sighted on the night of the thirtieth day,[11] the thirtieth day will be Rosh Chodesh.

If it is not sighted, Rosh Chodesh falls on the thirty-first day, while the thirtieth day is added to the previous month. There is no need to view the moon on the night of the thirty-first. Whether or

---

[6]   The solar year of 365 days is about 11 days longer than the lunar year which has 12 months of 29.5 days equaling 354 days.

[7]   In a cycle of nineteen years, seven years are intercalated to have thirteen months. They are every third, sixth, eighth, eleventh, fourteenth, seventeenth, and nineteenth year in the cycle.

[8]   Such as adding eleven days to the lunar year.

[9]   We do not count the number of days in measuring a year, but only the number of months (twelve). For example, if a person vows not to drink wine for a year, the prohibition for him not to drink wine ends on the same date the following year (twelve months later) even though it is eleven days short of a full 365-day solar year.

[10]   Conjunction occurs when the sun, the moon, and the earth are on a direct line; in other words, when the moon passes between the sun and the earth. At that point, the sun shines on the far side of the moon, and the side of the moon facing the earth is dark.

[11]   i.e., the night following the 29th day of the outgoing month. It is called the night of the thirtieth day, since the Halachic day starts at nightfall.

not the moon is seen, [the new month begins that night], because lunar months cannot be longer than thirty days.

THE FIXING OF ROSH CHODESH

1:4. When the moon is seen on the night of the thirtieth day resulting in a twenty-nine day month, the month is called *chaseir*— "lacking". If the moon is not sighted, and the previous month has thirty days, that month is called *me'ubar*—"pregnant" or *malei*— "full, prolonged".

When the moon is sighted on the thirtieth night, we say it was sighted at the expected time. When the moon is sighted on the thirty-first night, we say it has been sighted on the night of its fullness.

1:5. The [fixing of Rosh Chodesh] based on the sighting of the moon is not left to the discretion of each individual, as is the case with Shabbos where everyone counts six days and observes the seventh day as Shabbos. Rather, [the sanctification of the new month] has been delegated to the Sanhedrin[12]; the day they fix as Rosh Chodesh is Rosh Chodesh. For it says, . . . *This month will be for you*, meaning: the [evaluation of the] testimony [regarding the new moon] will be assigned to you, [Moshe, and the judges of the Sanhedrin who are like you].

1:6. The *Beis Din* figures [the hour when the new moon could appear] based on calculations of astronomers who know the positions of the stars and their orbits. They research carefully determining whether or not the moon could be seen at the expected time, i.e. the thirtieth night.

If the judges conclude that it is possible to sight [the moon], they sit and wait for witnesses [to testify] the entire thirtieth day. If

---

[12] The Supreme Court which was based in the Bais Hamikdash, while it stood.

witnesses do testify, and their testimony is verified, the court will sanctify the new month. If [the moon] was not seen, and witnesses do not come, the judges wait out the thirtieth day, thereby making the month *me'ubar* [prolonged].

If, according to their calculations, [the judges] know it is impossible for the moon to be seen the thirtieth night, they do not wait for witnesses to come. If witnesses do indeed come, we know they are either false witnesses or they saw a cloud that looked like, but was not, the moon.

1:7. It is a positive Torah commandment for *beis din* to figure out whether or not the moon will appear [on the thirtieth night]; to interrogate the witnesses until they verify their testimony; sanctify the new month, and dispatch [messengers] notifying the population on which day Rosh Chodesh was declared, so that they know [on which day to celebrate] Yom Tov, as it says, . . . *These are My fixed times, the fixed times of Hashem, which you shall proclaim as sacred holidays* (*Vayikra* 23:2), and, *This law must be kept at its designated time* (*Shemos* 13:10).[13]

1:8. The calculations and establishing of the months and leap years can be done only in Eretz Yisrael, for it says, *For the Torah will come forth from Zion, and the word of Hashem from Yerushalayim* (*Yeshayah* 2:3).

If a great sage who received *semichah*[14] in Eretz Yisrael left and no sage of equal eminence remained in Eretz Yisrael, he may make calculations, fix the date of Rosh Chodesh, and establish leap years outside Eretz Yisrael. However, if a sage as eminent as he arises in Eretz Yisrael—not to mention a sage of greater eminence—it is forbidden for him to fix the date of Rosh Chodesh and establish leap

---

[13] The verse which refers to the *korban Pesach*, tells us to bring it *at its designated time*, i.e., in the spring. It teaches us to establish leap years in order for Pesach to always fall in the spring.

[14] The process of ordination from sage to sage that began with Moshe ordaining Yehoshua and continued throughout the generations coming to a close in the 4th century c.e.

years outside Eretz Yisrael. If he transgresses and tries to regulate the calendar this way, his actions are null and void.

TESTIMONY OF WITNESSES

2:1. Only two males, fit to testify in all court cases can testify that they saw the new moon. Women and [Canaanite] slaves are unacceptable as witnesses and may not testify.

When a father and his son see the new moon they both go to testify. Not that they can act as joint witnesses, but if one of them is disqualified—because of thievery or some other reason—the other may join with another witness and testify.

One disqualified as a witness by rabbinic decree,[15] though not by Torah law, may not testify that he saw the new moon.

2:2. According to Torah law, there is no need to be overly particular regarding testimony about sighting the new moon. Even if the new month was sanctified based on the testimony of witnesses who later turned out to be false, the new month remains sanctified.

Originally, testimony about the appearance of the new moon was accepted from anyone [without checking his background], for we assume that any Jew is acceptable until it is known that he is unacceptable. But once the followers of Baitos[16] began to sabotage [the process], hiring people to testify they had seen the moon, when in fact they had not, the court decreed that it would only accept testimony from witnesses known to be impeccable, whose words were thoroughly probed.

2:3. Therefore, if the beis din [sanctifying the new moon] did not

---

15 For example, a gambler and one who lends money at interest.
16 Baitos and Tzadok (231 b.c.e.) were the founders of a deviant sect that believed only in the written Torah and rejected the oral Torah. Known as Tzedokim (Sadducees) and Baitosim (Boethusians), they greatly harassed the Torah-observant Jews of their time.

know the witnesses who sighted the moon, the citizens of the city where the new moon was sighted sent along other men to offer character references letting the judges know that these witnesses were trustworthy. Only then did the court accept their testimony.

2:4. The court made calculations based on astronomical computations. Thus they knew the position of the moon when it was sighted: whether it was to the north or south of the sun, whether its crescent was wide or narrow, and in what direction its tips were pointed.

When witnesses testified, the judges asked them, "Was the moon north or south of the sun?"

"In which direction were its tips pointed?"

"How high [above the horizon] and how wide did the moon seem to be?"

If their answers matched [the judges'] calculations, their testimony was accepted. If not, their testimony was not accepted.

2:5. If the witnesses said, they saw [the reflection of the moon] in water, or they saw the moon behind the clouds, in a mirror, or, they saw part of the moon in the sky and part of it behind the clouds, or, part of it reflected in water, or, part of it reflected in a mirror, such a sighting is not a valid basis for sanctifying the new month.

If one witness said, "The moon seemed to be two stories above the horizon," and the other witness said, "It was three stories high," their testimonies may be combined, [and the month sanctified, since we allow for a normal margin of error]. However, if one said, "It was three stories high," and the other said, "It was five stories high," their testimonies may not be combined, [because the difference is too great]. However, either of them may join with another witness giving the same testimony, or whose testimony differed by only one story.

2:6. If witnesses said, "We casually glanced at the moon, and afterwards, when focusing on it so we could testify we did not see it any more," their testimony is not valid for sanctifying the new month. For perhaps [they saw] a cloud formation that looked like the moon, which afterwards dispersed.

If witnesses said, "We saw the moon on the twenty-ninth day before sunrise in the east, and that evening, the night of the thirtieth, we saw it in the west," they are believed, and Rosh Chodesh may be sanctified on their testimony, because they saw the moon at the expected time [on the night of the thirtieth]. [Although, it is impossible to have seen the old moon the same morning the new moon is seen,] we disregard this part of their statement; assuming what they saw was a cloud that looked to them like the moon.

By the same token, if witnesses claim they saw the moon at the expected time [on the thirtieth night], yet it was not seen on the thirty-first night, their testimony is believed. We base our sanctification of the moon solely on the sighting [of the moon] on the night of the thirtieth.[17]

ACCEPTING THE TESTIMONY

2:7. What are the guidelines for accepting testimony about sighting the new moon?

Whoever saw the new moon and is fit to testify[18] comes to the beis din. A grand feast is prepared for the witnesses in a designated place to entice people to come. The pair [of witnesses] who arrive first are interrogated first with the questions mentioned above.[19] The elder witness is brought into [the judges' chamber] first and asked the questions. If his testimony conforms with the judges' own calculations, they invite his partner [to the chamber]. If their statements coincide, their testimony is valid.

The other pairs of witnesses are only asked the main points; [the beis din] does not need them, but in this way they will not leave

---

17 And assume the moon was not seen on the night of the thirty-first because its view was blocked by clouds.

18 Excluding a transgressor, a gambler, or a usurer.

19 In halachah 4.

disappointed, and will come again in the future [when their testimony may be needed].

2:8. After the witnesses' testimony is accepted, the head of the beis
din declares, "It is sanctified!" And all those present respond, "It is
sanctified! It is sanctified!"

At least three judges must sanctify the new month. Likewise, at
least three judges must calculate [the time of the new moon's ap-
pearance].

The month is sanctified only when the new moon is sighted at
its expected time [i.e., on the thirtieth night].

The new month is sanctified only during daytime. If it was sanctified at night, the sanctification is null and void.

Even if the beis din and the entire Jewish people saw the moon,
yet the beis din did not declare, "It is sanctified," before nightfall
beginning the thirty-first day; or if the witnesses were interrogated,
but the beis din was unable to declare afterwards, "It is sanctified"
before nightfall beginning the thirty-first day, the month is not sanctified and is declared prolonged. Despite the fact that the moon was
sighted on the thirtieth night, it is the thirty-first day that will be
Rosh Chodesh. For Rosh Chodesh is not established by the sighting of the moon, but by the beis din declaring, "It is sanctified!"

2:9. If the beis din themselves see the new moon at the end of the
twenty-ninth day, before a star has appeared on the thirtieth night,
the beis din may declare, "It is sanctified," because it is still day.[20]

If the judges see the new moon on the night of the thirtieth day
after two stars have appeared, [they proceed as follows:] In the
morning, two additional judges join one of the three original
judges [to form a beis din]. The other two original [judges] testify
before [this beis din] of three, who then [sanctify the new month].

2:10. Once the beis din sanctifies the new month, it remains sanc-

---

[20] Although the sun has set, the night does not begin until stars appear, and it is
therefore still possible to sanctify the new month.

tified, even if they erred inadvertently, or were misled [by false witnesses], or were forced to sanctify it. The dates of the festivals must be calculated based on the day that they sanctified [as Rosh Chodesh].

Even if one knows that [the beis din] erred, he is required to rely on them, for the matter is given over to them alone. The One who commanded us to observe the Yamim Tovim is the One who commanded us to rely on them, as it says, *These are My fixed times . . . which you shall proclaim . . .* (*Vayikra* 23:2).

TRAVEL ON SHABBOS TO TESTIFY

3:1. When witnesses see the new [moon], and within a day and a night they can reach the beis din, they should go to testify. If the distance is further, they should not go, because testimony after the thirtieth day is useless, since the month will already have been declared prolonged.

3:2. Witnesses who saw the new moon should travel to the beis din to testify even on Shabbos, for it says, *These are Hashem's festivals that you should proclaim* [*in their set times*] (*Vayikra* 23:2). Wherever the Torah uses the expression "set times", the prohibitions of Shabbos are set aside.

Therefore, the laws of Shabbos may be violated for the sake of Rosh Chodesh Nisan and Rosh Chodesh Tishri, so that the Yamim Tovim [Pesach, Yom Kippur, and Sukkos][21] can be celebrated at their proper times.

When the Beis Hamikdash was standing, [the laws of Shabbos] were set aside by every Rosh Chodesh, because the *musaf* offering that was brought on Rosh Chodesh, overrides the prohibitions of Shabbos.

---

21 The month of Sivan is not mentioned, because Shavuos is not celebrated on a particular date in the month Sivan, but at the conclusion of *Sefiras Ha'omer* which began on the second night of Pesach.

3:3. Just as the witnesses who saw the new moon violate the Shabbos [to testify], so too, the character witnesses [necessary] if the judges do not know the witnesses, violate the Shabbos.

Even if there is only one character witness, he accompanies them violating the Shabbos, because he may meet another person who can join him as a character witness.

3:4. If a witness who sighted the moon on Friday night is sick, he may be hoisted on a donkey [and carried to the beis din]. Even [if he is bedridden], his bed [may be transported] along with him.

If the witnesses are at risk of being ambushed en route,[22] they may carry weapons. If the distance to the beis din is great, they may take food with them.

Even if the moon was sighted as a large crescent, visible to everyone, one should not say, "Just as we saw the moon, so did others, therefore we need not violate the Shabbos." Rather everyone who saw the new moon, and is fit to testify and is within a day's travel to the beis din is obligated to violate the Shabbos and come to testify.

THE TWO DAYS OF ROSH HASHANAH

3:5. Originally, the beis din accepted testimony concerning the new moon the entire thirtieth day [until nightfall]. Once, the witnesses were delayed until late afternoon, causing confusion in the Beis Hamikdash.[23] For if they brought the afternoon sacrifice, and subsequently the witnesses arrived, [a problem would arise], for we may not bring the *musaf* offering [of Rosh Chodesh] after the daily afternoon sacrifice.[24]

---

[22] The Sadducees would lie in wait for the witnesses in order to delay their appearance in the beis din until after the thirtieth day.

[23] The Levites sang a psalm at the offering of the *nesachim* (drink offering) of the daily morning and afternoon sacrifices. In the present case witnesses had not arrived and the afternoon service had to be performed. Consequently, the Levites did not know whether to sing the weekday psalm or the Rosh Chodesh psalm, or no psalm at all.

[24] No offerings may be brought after the afternoon sacrifice is offered.

After that incident, the beis din made the following rule: Testimony regarding the new moon would be accepted only until the beginning of the afternoon, leaving enough time in the daylight hours to offer the *musaf* offerings, the daily afternoon sacrifice, and the drink offerings [that accompany them].

3:6. If the witnesses do not arrive by *minchah*, the daily afternoon sacrifice [alone] is brought. If witnesses arrive after *minchah* [of Rosh Hashanah], that day[25] [i.e., the thirtieth day of Elul] and the next day are kept as Yom Tov[26]. The *musaf* offering, however, is brought on the next day, because the new month is not sanctified after the time of *minchah*.

After the Beis Hamikdash was destroyed [and sacrifices were no longer offered], Rabbi Yochanan ben Zakkai and his beis din instituted to accept new moon testimony all day. Even if witnesses came immediately before sunset of the thirtieth day, their testimony is accepted and the thirtieth day alone is sanctified.

BONFIRES AND MESSENGERS

3:7. When the beis din decided that a month would be full because the witnesses did not appear the entire thirtieth day, they would go up to a pre-selected place and hold a feast on the thirty-first day which is *Rosh Chodesh*.[27]

They would not go up during the thirty-first night, but rather at daybreak, before sunrise. No fewer than ten [judges] would go up to this meal. It was essential that they serve at this meal bread made from grain and beans. Throughout halachic literature this meal is

---

[25] From sunset of the twenty-ninth day of Elul, the people were required to observe the day as if it were Rosh Hashanah, since from the next morning [i.e., the thirtieth] until the time of *minchah*, beis din might accept witnesses sanctifying the new month, and declaring the day as Rosh Hashanah.

[26] If the witnesses were not accepted on the thirtieth day, the next day is in reality Rosh Hashanah.

[27] The reason for the feast was to publicize that the month had been prolonged.

called "*se'udas mitzvah shel ibbur*—the mitzvah feast of the prolonged month."

3:8. Originally, when the beis din sanctified the new month they lit
bonfires on the mountaintops to convey [the news] to the people
in distant communities.[28] When the Samaritans began to sabotage
[the process] by lighting bonfires on the thirtieth day in order to
mislead the people [of the distant communities], the Sages ruled
that messengers be dispatched to notify the people.

These messengers may neither violate Yom Tov nor Shabbos,
[by traveling]. For one may only violate Shabbos [to report the
sighting of the new moon, to enable the beis din] to sanctify the
new month, not to announce its sanctification.

3:9. Six months a year messengers notified the [distant communi-
ties]: During Nisan because of Pesach; during Av because of the
fast [of *Tishah be'Av*]; during Elul, to anticipate the thirtieth day of
Elul because of Rosh Hashanah. If it became known to them that
the beis din sanctified the thirtieth day, they would observe only
the thirtieth day as Yom Tov. If not, they would observe both the
thirtieth and the thirty-first day as [Rosh Hashanah] until the messengers of Tishri arrived.[29]

[Messengers also travelled] during Tishri, because of the Yamim
Tovim; during Kislev because of Chanukah; during Adar because of
Purim. While the Beis Hamikdash was standing, messengers also
were sent out also during Iyar, because of the minor Pesach.[30]

3:10. [Even if the moon was clearly visible the previous night,]
messengers for the months of Nisan and Tishri did not travel on
Rosh Chodesh until the sun rose and they heard the beis din de-

---

[28] They signaled with strings of bonfires on mountain tops stretching in all direc-
tions.
[29] Until the messengers arrived on the thirty-first day and reported that Rosh
Hashanah was sanctified on the thirtieth day. Thus the thirty-first day is a weekday.
[30] Those who could not bring the *korban Pesach* on the day before Pesach were required to bring it on the fourteenth of Iyar (*Pesach sheini*).

clare, "It is sanctified."[31] However, if the messengers heard beis din sanctify Rosh Chodesh at the end of the twenty-ninth day, [before two stars appeared, which can happen,] as was explained [in 2:9], they may travel that evening.

However, during other months the messengers may travel in the evening after the moon has been sighted, although the beis din had not yet sanctified the new month; for *beis din* will surely sanctify the new month on the next day.

The Second Day of Yom Tov

3:11. Wherever these messengers arrived, [before Yom Tov began], the Yom Tov of that month was observed for one day only, as the Torah says. In distant communities which the messengers did not reach [before Yom Tov], the Yom Tov was observed for two days because they did not know which day the beis din fixed as Rosh Chodesh.

3:12. In some communities the messengers [who left during] Nisan arrived [in time for Pesach], but [during] Tishri they did not arrive [in time for Sukkos].[32] [These communities] should observe Pesach for one day, since the messengers reached them, and they knew which day was Rosh Chodesh [Nisan]. By the same token, they should observe Sukkos for two days, since the messengers had not reached them [in time for Sukkos]. However, to avoid differences between the Yamim Tovim, the Sages ruled that in all places the messengers for Tishrei did not arrive before Succos, two days should be observed [for all Yamim Tovim] even including the Yom Tov of Shavuos.[33]

---

[31] We do not rely on the assumption that Bais Din will surely sanctify the next day because the Yamim Tovim in these months are commanded by the Torah.

[32] Since the messengers for Tishrei were not allowed to travel on Rosh Hashanah and Yom Kippur.

[33] Shavuos is celebrated for two days, even though it is not tied to the date of Rosh Chodesh Sivan, being observed one day after the 49th day of the *Omer.*

3:13. [How much more time for travel] do these messengers for Nisan have than those for Tishri? Two days; because the messengers for Tishri do not travel on the first day of Tishri—[Rosh Hashanah] nor on the tenth—Yom Kippur.

3:14. There is no need for two messengers, because even a single individual is believed. In fact, any traveler who says, "I heard from the beis din that the new month was sanctified on such and such date," is believed, and the Yamim Tovim are celebrated accordingly. [Because one does not lie about] something that will eventually come to light, the testimony of a single qualified witness is acceptable.

BADGERING THE WITNESSES

3:15. If the beis din sat in session throughout the thirtieth day, but no witnesses arrived, and the judges arose early the next morning declaring the month as prolonged, as stated above [in halachah 3:7], and four or five days later—or even at the end of the month—witnesses from distant places came, testifying that they saw the new moon at the proper time, namely on the thirtieth night [so that the thirtieth day was actually Rosh Chodesh, the judges] intimidate the witnesses, bombarding them with questions, grilling them, and going over their words with a fine-tooth comb [trying to shake their testimony]. For the beis din does not want to sanctify the month [retroactively on the thirtieth,] after it has already been declared full.

3:16. However, if the witnesses testimony remains unshaken; and their words square [with the court's own calculations]; and the witnesses are well-known learned persons; and their testimony is verified, then the month is sanctified [retroactively]. The beis din revises the dates of the month, starting from the thirtieth day [of the previous] month, since the new moon was sighted on the night it was slated [to appear].

3:17. But if it was of crucial importance for the beis din to leave the month full, as, in fact, it was before the witnesses came, then it was indeed left full. This is the meaning of the statement, "The month is prolonged to meet an emergency."[34] There are eminent sages who disagree, believing the month should never be prolonged out of necessity. Rather, if witnesses arrive, they are heard without being intimidated, and the month is sanctified.

3:18. It seems to me that the Sages differ about this matter only in months other than Nisan and Tishri, or when witnesses arrive in Nisan and Tishri after the Yamim Tovim have passed. That being the case, the time to offer sacrifices and perform the [mitzvos of] Yom Tov passed.

However, when witnesses arrive in Tishri and Nisan before the middle of the month, [i.e., before Pesach and Sukkos], their testimony of sighting the moon at the proper time is accepted, and they are not intimidated. We do not browbeat the witnesses trying to nullify their testimony so that the month will remain full [without reason].

3:19. However, we do badger witnesses whose testimony is unclear and shaky, which might result in being disproved causing the month to be prolonged. We bear down on them [hoping to be able to accept] their testimony, in order that the month be sanctified in its proper time.

Similarly, if, additional witnesses [*mazimim*] arrive before the new month was sanctified, trying to overturn the testimony of the previous witnesses who testified that they saw the new moon at its proper time,[35] [the beis din] will intimidate those who want to

---

[34] *Rosh Hashanah* 20a. The emergency was to prevent Shabbos and Yom Kippur from falling on successive days. This was crucial because fresh vegetables would wilt and unburied corpses would begin to decompose if kept over two days.

[35] Following the rule of *hazama* which is that the testimony of witnesses can be nullified if a second pair of witnesses contradict the original testimony by claiming that the first pair of witnesses could not have been in the place where they claim to have seen the testimony because in fact they were together with the second group

overturn the original testimony, so that their accusation will not stand, and the new month can be sanctified at the proper time.

LEAP YEARS

4:1. A leap year is a year that has an extra month.[36] The extra month that is added is always Adar, so that a leap year has two months of Adar: the first and the second Adar.

Why is a month added? For with this addition, Pesach will fall in the spring, as it says, *Safeguard the month of springtime* (*Devarim* 16:1), [which is interpreted to mean:] Make sure the month [of Nisan] always falls in the spring. If the month [of Adar] was not added [periodically], some years Pesach would occur in the summer, and some years in the winter.

4:2. There are three factors which are considered when deciding if an extra month is to be added to the year:

1) so the beginning of the spring quarter (*tekufah*)[37] should be in the proper time,

2) so the early ripening grain should ripen in the proper time,

3) and so the fruit trees should blossom in the proper time.

How is this done? If the beis din realizes that the beginning of spring [the 21st of March] will fall on the 16th of Nisan or later,[38] a leap year is declared. The month that would have been Nisan becomes the second Adar, causing Pesach to fall in the spring.

---

in another place. The Torah says that in this situation, we accept the testimony of the second group and the original testimony is nullified. Here too, the *mazimim* come to invalidate the witnesses' testimony by saying that at the time they claimed to have seen the moon, they were together with them in a place other than where they claimed to have sighted the new moon.

[36] The extra month is added to adjust the lunar year to the solar year which is eleven days longer.

[37] The first day of spring, when the days and nights are equal, about March 21, also called the vernal equinox.

[38] Pesach begins on the 15th of Nisan.

This fact alone causes the beis din to make a leap year; no other considerations come into play.

4:3. So too, if the beis din sees that [the barley] crop has not ripened, rather it is late in sprouting, and the fruit trees that usually bloom around Pesach have not yet bloomed, the combination of these two signs are sufficient grounds to add an extra month, even if the beginning of spring (the 21st of March) will occur before the 16th of Nisan.

[This is done] so that there will be plenty of ripe [barley] available for the wave offering of the *omer* brought from barley on the sixteenth of Nisan, and so the fruit trees will sprout, as they should do, in the spring.

4:4. [Anticipating] the ripening of the barley crop, [the beis din] looks at three regions: Judea, the east bank of the Jordan, and the Galilee. If the barley ripened in two of these regions, the year is not made a leap year. But if [the barley] ripened in only one of these regions, the year is made a leap year if the fruit trees have not bloomed.

These are the main factors to consider when declaring a leap year, reconciling the lunar year with the solar year.

4:5. There are other reasons that prompt the beis din to declare a leap year in an emergency. They are:

The roads are impassable [because they are damaged by the rains], and the people cannot come to Yerushalayim [for the pilgrimage Yom Tov].[39] Making a leap year [allows time] for the rains to stop and the roads to be repaired.

The bridges have been washed away, and rivers are flooding the roads, making travel not only difficult but life-threatening.

The ovens[40] for [roasting] the *korban Pesach* were destroyed by

---

[39] It is a mitzvah for every male to celebrate Pesach, Shavuos and Sukkos in Yerushalayim (*Shemos* 23:13).

[40] Their ovens were made of clay, and at times were damaged by heavy rain.

the rains, thus the people will be unable to roast the *korban Pesach*. Making a leap year allows time to rebuild the ovens and have them dry [in the sun].

The Jews from the diaspora have left their homes but did not yet arrive in Yerushalayim. Making a leap year, enables them to reach [Yerushalayim before the Yom Tov].

4:6. We do not declare a leap year because of snow, because of cold weather, because Jews from the diaspora have not left their homes, or because of *tum'ah* (ritual impurity). For example, if most of the people or most of the kohanim are *tamei*, the year is not made a leap year so they can purify themselves before bringing the *korban Pesach*. Instead, they bring [the *korban Pesach*] while impure.[41] However, if erroneously the year was made a leap year because of ritual impurity, it remains a leap year.

4:7. There other factors which are not sufficient cause for declaring a leap year, yet, serve as additional reasons for making a leap year when a leap year is declared so that [Pesach would fall] after the *tekufah*, or so [the barley will be] ripe, and the fruit trees [will blossom].

These are the [secondary] reasons: Few young goats or lambs have been born, or the young pigeons have not [grown enough to] fly.

We do not make a leap year so goats and lambs will be available for the Pesach offerings, or pigeons will be available for the Yom Tov or other obligatory sacrifices. However, these facts are mentioned as additional reasons for making a leap year.

4:8. How does the beis din use [these factors] as additional reasons for making a leap year?

The beis din declares: "This year must be made a leap year because the *tekufah* [the first day of spring] falls late, or because the [barley] has not ripened and the fruit trees are not yet blooming,

---

[41] Following the rule that when a majority of the people or the kohanim are impure, the Pesach sacrifice may be brought.

and—additionally—because the young goats are small and the pigeons are still tender."

THE VOTING PROCESS

4:9. Only [judges] invited to take part in the conference [on this subject] can declare a leap year. How is this done? The head of the High Court invites members of the Sanhedrin saying, "You are invited to such-and-such location where we will decide whether it is necessary to declare a leap year." Only invited judges are authorized to make a leap year.

How many [judges are invited to the conference] on making a leap year? Though seven judges are invited, we begin the discussion with three judges from the High Court who have received semicha.[42] If two [of these judges] say, "We don't need a conference on making a leap year," [their opinion is decisive], and the opinion of the dissenting judge is overruled.

If two [of these judges] say, "We should investigate the matter," with one judge disagreeing, two of the originally invited judges are added to the court, and [five] judges open debate on the subject.

4:10. If two [of the five judges] are in favor of a leap year while three vote against it, the two are outvoted. If three [judges] favor making a leap year, with two against it, the remaining two [judges] are added to the court, to debate the matter.

These seven [judges] make the final determination, and their decision is binding. If there is a difference of opinion among them, we follow the majority.

The head of the High Court, who presides over the seventy-one [judges of the Sanhedrin], must be one of these seven judges. If the three [original judges] decided to declare a leap year, their procla-

---

42 *Semichah* (ordination) was granted from one generation to the next, going back to the days of Moshe who gave *semichah* to Yehoshua (*Devarim* 34:9).

mation is valid, provided the *nasi* (the head of the court) is one of the three, or he agrees with their decision.

Junior judges are the first to express their opinions when deliberating about a leap year.[43] In contrast, when we sanctify the new month, we begin with the head of the court.[44]

4:11. Neither the king nor the *Kohen Gadol* should be on the board which debates the need for a leap year. Because a king may be swayed by factors relating to his army[45] and wars, and the *Kohen Gadol*, mindful that he has to immerse five times, on Yom Kippur may be averse to declaring a leap year so that Tishri will not fall in the chilly [winter weather].

4:12. If the *nasi*—head of the supreme *beis din*—is away, [the beis din] may declare a leap year, conditionally. If the *nasi* approves when he returns, it is a leap year. If not, it is not a leap year.

A leap year may be declared in the territory of Yehudah (Judea) only, since that is where [the Beis Hamikdash,]—the dwelling place of the *Shechinah*—is located. As it says, *It is there that you shall go and seek His Presence* (*Devarim 12:5*).

[Even so,] if a leap year is enacted in the Galilee, it remains a leap year. One can only declare a leap year during the day. It is not valid if it is done during the night.

4:13. The beis din has the power to calculate and determine which year should be a leap year, even several years in advance. Nevertheless, a specific year is not declared a leap year until after Rosh Hashanah, with an announcement stating, "This year is a leap year."[46]

---

[43] If the elder judges would speak first, the junior judges would be overawed by the arguments of the high-ranking judges and be reluctant to express their own opinion.
[44] Because this is just a ritual whereby the head of the court pronounces the month as sanctified.
[45] The king paid his soldiers an annual salary. By adding an extra month to the year, he would save one month's pay (Rashi on *Sanhedrin* 18b).
[46] If beis din declared before Rosh Hashanah that a second Adar would be added six month later, it may be forgotten, and people may eat *chametz* on Pesach (Rashi, *Sanhedrin* 12a).

[The announcement is made at such an early date] only in an emergency.[47] If there is no emergency, the announcement is not made until Adar. At that time the beis din proclaims the present year a leap year, and the next month the second Adar, rather than Nisan.

4:14. A proclamation before Rosh Hashana does not make the year a leap year. Once the thirtieth day of Adar is reached without a proclamation of a leap year, they may not do so, because the thirtieth day can become the first day of Nisan and we have a rule that once we enter the month of Nisan we may not make a leap year. However, if a leap year was declared on the thirtieth of Adar, their ruling remains in effect.

If witnesses arrive after the leap year was declared, testifying that they saw the new moon, the beis din sanctifies the new month on the thirtieth day, making that day Rosh Chodesh of the second Adar. Had they sanctified the new month [as Nisan] on the thirtieth day [of Adar], before declaring a leap year, they would no longer be able to declare a leap year, since a leap year may not be declared in Nisan.

4:15. We do not declare a leap year during famine because it is impossible to extend the prohibition of using new produce for another month, when everyone is anticipating opening the storehouses for the new produce.[48]

We do not make the Sabbatical year a leap year, since everyone has the right to the crops that grow by themselves. [Were it] a leap year, there might not be enough grain for the *omer* offering [on the sixteenth of Nisan] and for the two loaves of bread [offered on Shavuos].[49]

---

[47] For fear that the Romans, in an attempt to disrupt the Jewish calendar, may forbid instituting a leap year.

[48] The Torah forbids eating grain from the new crop (*chadash*) until the *omer* is offered on the sixteenth of Nisan (*Vayikra* 23:14). In a famine, extending this prohibition for a month would create great hardship.

[49] Since these must come from the new crop.

Usually the year preceding the Sabbatical year was made a leap year.[50]

4:16. It seems to me, that when the Sages say we do not declare a leap year during a famine or in a Sabbatical year, they mean when a leap year is declared because of roads or bridges that are in need of repair. But if declaring a leap year is called for because [Pesach will fall before] the beginning of spring [i.e., 21st of March], or because [the barley has not] ripened, and the fruit trees have not blossomed, then we will declare a leap year, [even in years of famine or in a Sabbatical year].

4:17. When the beis din declares a leap year, they send letters to all the distant communities notifying them that a leap year has been enacted and the reason for this enactment.

These letters were written in the name of the *nasi*, stating:

"This is to inform you that I and my colleagues have agreed to add to this year, this many days". [The reason they don't say we have added an extra month is] because the beis din has the right to add a month of 29 or 30 days. [This was determined on the basis of astronomical calculations] which benefitted the people in the outlying regions. However, the actual decision as to whether the month has 29 or 30 days is based on the sighting of the new moon.

THE FIXED CALENDAR

5:1. Fixing Rosh Chodesh based on sighting the moon, and establishing leap years to reconcile the calendar with the seasons or for another necessity, applies only to the *Sanhedrin* in Eretz Yisrael. Only they, or a court of ordained judges, granted authority by the *Sanhedrin*, and holding session in Eretz Yisrael [may make these decisions].

---

[50] To give the farmers an extra month to bring in the crops in advance of the Sabbatical year.

[The Sages derive this] from the command given to Moshe and Aharon, "*This month shall be for you the beginning of the months*" (*Shemos* 12:2). The Oral Torah, passed down from teacher to student, beginning with Moshe Rabbeinu, explains the words ["shall be for you"] as follows:[51] This testimony is handed over to you [in your capacity as Sanhedrin] and those [sages] who succeed you in this capacity.

When there is no *Sanhedrin* in Eretz Yisrael, we establish the monthly calendar and declare leap years according to the fixed calendar that we use today.

5:2. This ruling is a halachah given to Moshe on Mount Sinai. When there is a *Sanhedrin*, Rosh Chodesh is declared on the basis of visual sighting [of the new moon]. When there is no *Sanhedrin*, Rosh Chodesh is fixed according to the calendar we use today, paying no attention to visual sighting.

When the pre-set calendar is followed, Rosh Chodesh may be on the day which the new moon is sighted, or a day before or after the sighting of the new moon. It is rare for [the calendrical] Rosh Chodesh to be the day after the sighting [of the new moon, happening only] in countries west of Eretz Yisrael.[52]

5:3. When did the entire Jewish people begin using this calendar? At the end of the Talmudic era, when Eretz Yisrael lay in ruin, and an established court was no longer in operation. During the eras of the Mishnah and Gemara until the time of Abaye and Rava,[53] [the people] relied on the fixing [of Rosh Chodesh] in Eretz Yisrael.

---

[51] See *Rosh Hashanah* 21b.
[52] For in countries west of Eretz Yisrael the moon appears earlier than in Eretz Yisrael.
[53] who lived in Babylonia in the later period of the Amoraim.

ONE DAY OR TWO DAYS YOM TOV

5:4. When the *Sanhedrin* existed and Rosh Chodesh was declared based on sighting the new moon, the people in Eretz Yisrael and those residing in places the messengers of Tishri could reach, celebrated Yamim Tovim for one day only.

People living in places that could not be reached by the messengers of Tishri, celebrated two days, because they did not know which day the Sanhedrin in Eretz Yisrael fixed as Rosh Chodesh.

5:5. Nowadays, when the *Sanhedrin* and the beis din of Eretz Yisrael no longer exist, Rosh Chodesh is set according to the fixed calendar. We might expect Jews throughout the world to observe Yom Tov for one day only, for those who live in Eretz Yisrael and outside Eretz Yisrael rely on the same fixed calendar. Yet, the Sages decreed that [the people living outside Eretz Yisrael] should keep up the custom of their ancestors [observing the *Yom Tov sheini shel galuyos*, the second day Yom Tov of the *galus*].

5:6. Therefore, [people living in] the places the messengers of Tishri could not reach—in the days when messengers were dispatched—observe two days even at the present time, just as they did when the people of Eretz Yisrael declared Rosh Chodesh based on visually sighting the new moon.

At the present time, the people living in Eretz Yisrael keep their custom of celebrating one day, since they never celebrated two days. Thus, our observance of the second day of Yom Tov in the diaspora is a Rabbinic ordinance.

5:7. [Even] when Rosh Chodesh was fixed on the basis of visual sighting, most people in Eretz Yisrael celebrated Rosh Hashanah for two days, because they did not know which day beis din had declared as Rosh Chodesh, since the messengers did not leave on the Yom Tov [of Rosh Hashanah].

5:8. Even in Yerushalayim, Rosh Hashanah was observed two days many times.[54] For if witnesses did not arrive on the thirtieth day [after Rosh Chodesh Elul], the day on which they awaited [the arrival of] witnesses was regarded as holy, as well as the following day.

Since [there were times when] they observed [Rosh Hashanah for] two days even when beis din declared Rosh Chodesh based on sighting the new moon, the Sages decreed that even the Jews of Eretz Yisrael observe [Rosh Hashanah] for two days.

We now understand that even the observance of the second day of Rosh Hashanah today is rabbinically ordained.

5:9. The decision if a place should celebrate Yom Tov for one or two days is not solely dependent on its distance [from Yerushalayim].

A place may be located within a five-day journey or less from Yerushalayim, thus it was surely possible for the messengers to reach it, yet we can not say they should observe only one day. For we do not know if the messengers of beis din traveled to this place. Perhaps no Jews lived there at that time. [And if] Jews settled there only after the permanent calendar came into use, they observe two days.

Or, [perhaps the messengers did not go there] because bandits set road blocks, as happened between Yerushalayim and the Galilee in the days of the Mishnah; or perhaps the Samaritans prevented the messengers from passing through their territory.

5:10. If the matter hinged solely on distance in miles, the Jews of Egypt would observe the Yamim Tovim for only one day, for the messengers of Tishri can easily reach them, because, the distance from Yerushalayim to Egypt by way of Ashkelon can be covered in eight days or less. The same holds true for most of Syria. This proves[55] that the matter is not contingent on distance alone.

---

[54] From sunset after the twenty-ninth day of Elul they observed the day as if it were Rosh Hashanah, because *beis din* might accept witnesses and declare Rosh Hashanah the following morning.

[55] For everyone knows that the Jews of Egypt and Syria keep two days.

5:11. To sum up the main points:

Whenever it takes more than ten days to travel from Yerushalayim to a given place, its residents should observe the Yom Tov for two days, as they always did. For messengers sent out for Tishri can only reach places that are within a ten-day journey from Yerushalayim.[56]

[The following rules apply] to places that are a ten-day journey or less from Yerushalayim, thus possible for messengers to reach them: If the place is located in the portions of Eretz Yisrael conquered in the second conquest inhabited by Jews during the time the months were established by the sighting of the moon—for example, Usha, Sh'faram, Luz, Teveriah, and the like—[the residents] should observe only one day.

If the place is part of Syria—for example, Tyra, Damascus, Ashkelon, and the like—they should follow the custom of their ancestors. If [their custom was to celebrate] one day, they celebrate one day; if two days, they celebrate two days.

5:12. When a place is located within a journey of ten days or less from Yerushalayim, and it is part of Syria or the diaspora, and [its residents] have no set custom, they should observe two days, as is customary of the world at large. [The same rules apply to] a city newly created in the desert of Eretz Yisrael, or a city that we know was first settled by Jews in the present time. Observance of the second day of Yom Tov is a Rabbinic ordinance, even the second day of Rosh Hashanah although it is observed everywhere.

5:13. The calculations people make nowadays to figure out which day is Rosh Chodesh and which day is Yom Tov in their community do not designate the new month and it is not what we rely on. For we cannot institute leap years or declare Rosh Chodesh outside Eretz Yisrael.

We make the calculations just for convenience. For we know

---

[56] They do not travel on Rosh Hashanah, Yom Kippur, and the two Saturdays between Rosh Hashanah and Sukkos.

that the people of Eretz Yisrael rely on the same calculations. Thus, our calculations are meant to determine the day that the people of Eretz Yisrael will establish as Rosh Chodesh or as Yom Tov. For it is the fixing of Rosh Chodesh or a Yom Tov by the people of Eretz Yisrael that is decisive, not our calculations of the calendar.

CALCULATING THE APPEARANCE OF THE NEW MOON

11:1. As mentioned earlier, the beis din made accurate calculations and knew whether or not the new moon would appear [on a given night]. Therefore anyone with the proper intention who thirsts for words of wisdom and delves into mysteries, will want to know the method of calculation so he can determine if the new moon will be visible on a particular night.

11:2. There are many differences of opinion among the ancient gentile astronomers and mathematicians about the methods of calculation. Great scientists have erred regarding these matters. Unaware of certain facts, they were seized by doubts.

Even after many calculations, they have not been able to figure out when the moon becomes visible. "They dived into the mighty waters and brought up a potsherd in their hands.[57]"

11:3. Over the course of history, after a great deal of research, other scientists have discovered the correct formula. We also have traditions from our Sages regarding these principles, and [we have] proofs that were never published. Therefore, I thought it advisable to describe a method of calculation usable for anyone interested in this field.

11.4. Don't take these calculations lightly, thinking that they are not relevant today, for these formulas are complex and profound

---

[57] An expression borrowed from *Bava Kamma* 91a.

matters, comprising the *sod ha'ibbur*, "the mystery of the birth of the new moon" which was known only to great sages. This secret was only revealed to ordained and insightful [wise men].

However, nowadays when beis din does not fix the months based on the testimony of witnesses, the calculations used for our calendar are [a simple matter that] even school children can understand in three or four days.

11:5. A gentile or Jewish scientist who studied Greek wisdom, may detect slight inaccuracies when pondering my system of calculating the appearance of the moon. Do not think I am unaware of this approximation.

However, since this estimation did not affect the knowledge of the timing of the new moons appearance, it is immaterial, and therefore I was not exact.

11:6. Similarly, minor discrepancies in the system of computation were done on purpose. For our system has certain advantages which, ultimately, produce a correct result without lengthy computations. Thus, a person unfamiliar with such things will not be distracted by knotty computations actually useless in terms of the moon's visibility.

EMPIRICAL PROOFS

17:24. The principles on which these calculations are based, and the reasons why a given number is added or subtracted, how all these concepts are known, and the proofs for each of these principles, are all outlined in the numerous books on astronomy written by the Greeks. Their books can be found in scholarly libraries.

The books [about astronomy] written by the Jewish Sages of the tribe of Yissachar[58] who lived in the age of the prophets have not

---

[58] The sages of the tribe of Yissachar specialized in calculating the calendar, as it says, "The descendants of Yissachar were men who knew how to interpret the signs of the times" (1 *Divrei Hayamim* 12:33).

been transmitted to us. But since all these theories can be verified by indisputable scientific proofs, we do not care whether the author is a prophet or a non-Jewish astronomer. When a theory has been verified by sound empirical proofs, we do not rely on the authority of the scientist who advanced the theory but on the evidence of the experiments that substantiate the concept.

SUMMARY

19:16. And so we have explained all the calculations that are needed [to determine the time of the] sighting [of the moon] and for the examination of the witnesses. [We have described them in a way] that makes everything clear to knowledgeable people, so that they will fully understand how the Torah solves these problems. This way they will not have to look for answers in non-Jewish books. *"Search and read it in the Book of Hashem—not one of these is missing"* (*Yeshayah* 34:16).

HILCHOS TAANIYOS
LAWS OF FAST DAYS

———◆———

PRAYER AND SOUNDING OF TRUMPETS

1:1. It is a positive commandment of the Torah to publicly cry out [in prayer] and to sound the trumpets when any tragedy strikes the community, as it says, "*When you go to war in your land against an enemy who oppresses you, you shall sound the trumpets*" (*Bamidbar* 10:9).

[This commandment is not limited to war alone,] but whenever disaster strikes—including famine, plague, locusts, or the like—we should cry out, praying to God, and sounding the trumpets.

1:2. This is done to bring the people to do *teshuvah*. For when a tragedy occurs and people cry out to God, sounding trumpets, everyone understands that [the tragedy] came about because of their sins, as it says, "*Your sins have withheld the bounty from you*" (*Yirmeyah* 5:25). This will help to remove the calamity.

1:3. If people don't cry out and sound the trumpets, considering this calamity to be a natural occurrence, they are callous.[59] [Their outlook] prompts them to keep up their sinful ways, thus bringing on themselves more tragedy.

———

[59] They deny that God brought about the mishap as an act of kindness which ultimately will benefit them. Instead, they say that the disaster is the result of the cold, uncaring laws of nature.

This is implied in the verse, *"If you remain indifferent to Me, then I will act against you with wrathful hostility"* (*Vayikra* 6:27-28) which means: When I bring adversity on you in order to make you repent, and you say that it is merely an accident, then I will add the element of hostility to the [punishment] for your indifference [to Divine Providence][60].

COMMUNAL FAST DAYS

1:4. [In addition to praying and sounding the trumpets,] it is a Rabbinic enactment to fast whenever distress strikes the community, [continuing the fasts] until there is a sign of Divine mercy, [and the distress passes].

On these fast days we cry out in prayer, pleading and sounding only trumpets [without accompaniment of the shofar].

In the *Beis Hamikdash* both the trumpets and the shofar were sounded. The shofar blasts were short, while the trumpet blasts were drawn out longer [than the shofar blasts], since the mitzvah of the day is with trumpets. The trumpets can be sounded together with the shofar only in the *Beis Hamikdash*, for it says, *"With trumpets and the blasts of the shofar raise a shout before Hashem, the King"* (*Tehillim* 98:6).

1:5. Communal fast days called because of distressful conditions, should not be held on consecutive days, since the community cannot endure it.

Communal fasts should be held only on a Monday, the following Thursday, and the Monday after that. This sequence—Monday, Thursday, Monday—should be continued until God mercifully [lifts the hardship].

1:6. Communal fast days should not be set on Shabbos or Yom

---

[60] The word "keri" is the Hebrew root for both the word indifferent and hostility, pointing out that wrathful hostility is the proper punishment for indifference.

Tov. On these days, neither a shofar nor a trumpet should be blown, nor do we cry out, imploring God in our prayers.

The only exceptions are if a city is surrounded by [hostile] non-Jewish forces, or threatened by an overflowing river, or a ship is sinking at sea, [because these are life-threatening situations]. [In these cases,] and even when a single individual is being chased by gentiles, by robbers, or possessed by an evil spirit,[61] (we may fast on Shabbos,) cry out to God, and implore Him for [the victim's] sake. However, trumpets should not be blown for him, unless they are sounded [as an alarm] to round up people to come to save his life.

1:7. Similarly, a fast should not be declared on *Rosh Chodesh*, *Chanukah*, *Purim*, or *Chol Hamo'ed*. However, if the community has begun to fast, even for a single day because of a distressful situation, and the schedule of fasts [Monday, Thursday, Monday] requires that a fast be held on one of the above-mentioned days, they should fast for the entire day completing the fast.

1:8. Pregnant women, nursing mothers and children do not fast on communal fasts that are called because of a calamity.

We are allowed to eat the night before all these fasts, except those called for [lack of] rain, as will be explained further on. One may eat until dawn, provided he does not sleep. If one does sleep, he may not eat after getting up.[62]

PRIVATE FASTS

1:9. Just as a community fasts when disaster strikes, so too an individual should fast when struck by adversity. For example, if one's

---

[61] i.e., he became insane and may harm himself (*Rashi, Taanis* 22b).
[62] According to the *Shulchan Aruch, Orach Chaim* 564:1, one who resolves before going to sleep to get up before dawn and eat, is allowed to eat, and his fast still counts as a fast.

relative or friend is sick, lost in the desert, or imprisoned, one should fast for his sake, pray for mercy, and insert the *Aneinu*[63] prayer in each daily *Shemoneh esrei*. One should not fast on Shabbos, Yom Tov, Rosh Chodesh, Chanukah, or Purim.

1:10. An individual must accept a fast upon himself before sunset [of the previous day], for it to be considered valid. How does one accept a fast? After praying *Minchah* he says, "Tomorrow I will fast," mentally obligating himself to do so. It does not matter that he ate at night.

Similarly, one may obligate himself to fast for three or four consecutive days, yet eat each intervening night. It is not necessary to restate one's intent on the afternoon before each ensuing day.

1:11. If one undertook to fast, and the night [after completing his fast] he decided to continue fasting the following day, though he fasted overnight, it is not considered as a fast, because he did not commit himself to fast while it was still day. Certainly, if he ate and drank at night, deciding to continue his fast [upon awakening], it is not considered a fast.

1:12. A person who had a frightening dream must fast on the following day, to motivate himself to mend his way of life, examining his actions, and doing *teshuvah*. One fasts [a "bad dream fast"] even on Shabbos, and he inserts the *Aneinu* prayer in each *Shemoneh esrei*. [This holds true] even though he did not commit himself to fast on the previous day.

When one fasts on Shabbos, he must fast on yet another day, [to atone for] transgressing the mitzvah of taking delight in Shabbos [which includes enjoying three meals].

1:13. A person may fast for several hours [although he did not commit himself to fast the previous day], provided he does not eat anything the rest of the day. What does this mean? [An example:]

---

[63] The special prayer pleading God to answer us on our fasts.

A person was involved in business and did not eat until noon or even later that afternoon. He may decide to fast the rest of the day, fasting and inserting the *Aneinu* in the *Shemoneh esrei* of *Minchah*, since he committed himself to fast before beginning it. If he ate or drank and then began to fast for the remainder of the day, it is also a "fast of hours"

1:14. Whenever a person fasts, whether because of a personal setback, an alarming dream, or a calamity that befell the community, he should not feel at ease, be cheerful, or in a good mood. Rather, he should be somber and mournful, as it says, "*Of what shall a living man complain? Each one of his own sins*" (*Eichah* 3:39).

[A person who is fasting] is permitted to sample up to a *revi'is*[64] of food, provided he spits it out without swallowing it. If he forgot and ate, he should still complete his fast.

1:15. If one is fasting for a sick person, and the patient recovers, or because of a grave situation, and the trouble passes, he should complete his fast.

A person who travels from a place where [the community] is fasting to a place where [the community] is not fasting, should complete his fast. When he travels from a place where [the community] is not fasting to a place where [the community] is fasting he should fast together with them. If he forgets and does eat and drink, he should not show his contentment and gratification publicly.

1:16. When a community fasts because of drought, and rain begins to fall before noon, they should not complete their fast. Rather, they should eat and drink, assembling afterwards to read the *Great Hallel*,[65] which is only recited when one is content and replete with food.

---

[64] According to Rabbi Moshe Feinstein, a *revi'is* is 4.42 fluid ounces for Torah-ordained mitzvos, e.g. the quantity of wine to drink for the first cup at the *seder*; with regard to *mitzvos d'Rabbonon*—as in the case of eating *maror* at the *seder*, a *revi'is* is 1.1 fluid ounces, or a minimum of .7 fluid ounces.

[65] The *Great Hallel* is chapter 136 in *Tehillim*.

If [the rains came] after midday, they should complete their fast, since most of the day has passed in holiness. [The same rules apply] if [a community] was fasting because of a distressful situation, or harsh decree; if relief came before noon, they need not complete their fast; [if relief came] after midday, they should complete their fast.

1:17. Whenever a communal fast is proclaimed because of a distressing event, the [local] court and elders convene in the synagogue after *Shacharis* prayer until noon, reviewing the conduct of the city's residents, in order to remove the stumbling blocks that caused [the people to] sin. They warn the people, investigating all the sinners, [persuading them to] mend their ways and [seek] the people who terrorize the populace putting them to shame.

During the third quarter of the day they read the blessings and the curses in the Torah,[66] as it says, "*Do not reject the discipline of Hashem, my son, and do not abhor His rebuke*" (*Mishlei* 3:11). The *haftarah* they read is a portion from the prophets pertaining to the distress [for which they are fasting].[67] During the [fourth] quarter of the day, *Minchah* is recited, and [the people] offer supplications, cry out [to God] and confess, each according to his ability.

When Should a Communal Fast Be Declared?

2:1. A communal fast should be proclaimed and trumpets should be sounded in the following situations:

because of the distress the Jew-haters cause the Jews;

because of [the passage] of a military force;

because of a plague;

because of a beast [running wild];

---

[66] The *Tochachah* (the blessings and curses) in *parashas Bechukosai* (*Vayikra*, chapter 26). Our *minhag* is to read *Vayechal Moshe* (*Shemos* 32:11-14, 34:1-10), as on all public fasts.

[67] Our *minhag* is to read the *haftarah* of *Dirshu Hashem behimotze'o* (*Yeshayah* 55:6), as on all public fasts.

because of locusts;
because of chewing locusts;
because of the black blight;
because of the yellow blight;
because of collapsing buildings;[68]
because of an epidemic;
because of [the loss of the source of] sustenance,
and because of [the lack of] rain.

2:2. [The inhabitants of] a city stricken by any of these adversities should fast, sounding the trumpets until the disaster passes. The people surrounding the vicinity also fast but do not sound the trumpets. However, they should pray for mercy for their [afflicted neighbors]. We do not cry out [to God] or sound the trumpets on Shabbos, as was explained,[69] except if the tragedy is [the loss of the source of] sustenance. In that case we do cry out [to God] even on Shabbos, though we do not sound the trumpets.

2:3. What is meant by "the distress the Jew-haters cause the Jews"?

When non-Jews wage war against the Jews, [or they single out Jews] for special taxation, or they seize land from them or issue a decree [forbidding the observance of], even a [seemingly] minor mitzvah, we should fast and sound the trumpets until God has mercy.

All nearby cities should fast too, though they only blow trumpets if it is necessary as an alarm to round up people to come to their aid.[70]

2:4. What is meant by "[the passage of] a military force"?

This applies even to a military force that marches with peaceful intentions, such as a foreign army passing through Jewish territory on their way to fight against another nation. Although they are not

---

[68] and the earthquakes that cause them to collapse.
[69] Chapter 1:6.
[70] see chapter 1:6.

at war with the Jews, this is still considered a time of distress for which we should fast, as it says, [in one of the blessings,] *"and no sword shall cross your land"* (*Vayikra* 26:6). This implies that seeing war is itself a cause for distress.

2:5. "Because of a plague." When [is a sickness] considered a plague? Sickness is a plague when three people die on three consecutive days in a city that has 500 male inhabitants. It is not a plague if [three people] die on one day or on four days.

If a city has 1,000 male inhabitants, and six people die on three consecutive days, it is considered a plague. If [six people] die on one day or on four days, it is not considered a plague. This proportion [of 500:3, 1000:6] should be applied [to all cities, regardless of size].

Women, children, and older men who no longer work are not included in the count [to determine a plague].[71]

2:6. If there is a plague in Eretz Yisrael, Jews outside Eretz Yisrael should fast for the sake [of their endangered fellow—Jews]. If there is a plague in one country, but caravans frequently travel from there to another country, the inhabitants of both countries should fast, even if they are far apart.

2:7. We do not fast because of a wild animal unless it is mad.[72] How do we determine this? If it is seen in a city during the day, it is mad. If it is seen in a field during the day encountering two men without fleeing from them, it is mad. If the animal was in a field close to a swamp, and it saw two men and chased them, it is mad. If it did not chase them, it is not mad.

If the beast was in a swamp, it is not considered mad even if it

---

[71] Since women, children, and elderly men are more susceptible to disease than adult males, it is only when a number of adult males die that we can determine that a disease is a plague.

[72] The Hebrew *meshulachas*, "sent from Heaven" implies that the animal is acting in an abnormal way.

chased them, unless it killed both of them and ate [only] one.[73] If it ate both of them in a swamp, it is not considered mad, for [the swamp] is its territory, and it killed them because it was hungry, not because it was mad.

2:8. When houses are built in a desert or in unpopulated regions, which are the natural habitat for wild beasts, an animal is only considered mad when it climbs on a roof and takes a baby from a cradle. Otherwise it is not considered mad. [The blame rests] on the people who risked their lives by coming to a place where wild animals live.

2:9. When a throng of swarming animals like snakes or scorpions, or swarms of hornets, mosquitos and the like strike, we do not fast and sound the trumpets because of them. We do, however, cry out to God without blowing the trumpets.

2:10. "Because of locusts and chewing locusts." Even if only one specimen is seen in all of Eretz Yisrael, [the entire country] should fast and blow the trumpets because [locusts multiply rapidly]. [This rule applies if] even the smallest number of *govai* [a kind of locust] appear. However, for *chagav*—[which are smaller and less voracious],—we do not fast or blow the trumpets, but we do cry out to God.

2:11. "Because of the black blight and the yellow blight." As soon as these blights strike the crops, a fast is proclaimed and the trumpets are blown, even if only [an area as small as the size of] the opening of an oven is affected.

2:12. "Because of collapsing buildings." When a number of strong walls in a city that are not standing on the banks of rivers are collapsing, [the people] are faced with a calamity that calls for fasting and the blowing of trumpets.

---

[73]   The fact that it ate only one man shows that it was not driven by hunger, but by madness.

Similarly, we should fast and sound the trumpets because of earthquakes and hurricanes that destroy buildings and kill people.

2:13. When [is sickness] an epidemic? When a sickness, such as croup or paralysis, strikes many people in a city, causing them to die, it is considered a universal affliction that calls for fasting and the sounding of the trumpets.

Similarly, if the majority of a community is stricken with a skin disease, the affliction is regarded as boils, and the people should fast and sound the trumpets. For a dry itch [which has spread through the entire community,] we merely cry out [to God].

2:14. What is meant by "because of [the loss] of sustenance"? When the price of products that provide income for the majority of people in a city—such as linen in Babylonia and wine and oil in Eretz Yisrael—declines 60%, it is considered a universal calamity that calls for shouting and crying out to God, even on Shabbos.

2:15. What is meant by "because of rain"? When it rains heavily enough to cause flooding, [the community] should offer prayers. There is no greater calamity than having homes collapse, becoming graves [for the people living in them].

In *Eretz Yisrael* we do not pray for heavy rains to end. It is a mountainous country, and the homes are made of stone. Heavy rains benefit [the country], and we do not fast to remove something good.

2:16. [If it rained, and] the grain sprouted, then the rains stopped, and the sprouts begin to dry, the people should fast and cry out [to God] until it rains again or the crop dries out altogether, [so that fasting would be pointless].

Similarly, if the Pesach season—when trees should bloom in Eretz Yisrael—arrived, yet it does not rain,[74] the people should fast

---

74 And the rain is needed for the fruit to grow.

and cry out [to God] until the rain that is needed for the trees falls, or until the season passes.

2:17. Similarly, if Sukkos arrived and not enough rain has fallen to fill the storage tanks, the irrigation ditches, and the caves, the people should fast until it rains enough to fill them.

If there is a shortage of drinking water, they should fast for rain even in the summer [although it is not the rainy season].

2:18. A drought is declared if it began raining during the rainy season and then stopped for more than forty days. People should fast and cry out [to God] until the rains come or until the rainy season passes.

FASTS FOR RAIN

3:1. If it does not rain at all at the beginning of the rainy season, [the following agenda is observed]:

If it does not rain by the seventeenth of Marcheshvan, the Torah scholars should begin to fast, on Monday, the following Thursday and the following Monday. All yeshivah students may consider themselves worthy of fasting.

3:2. If it does not rain by *Rosh Chodesh* Kislev, the *beis din* decrees three communal fasts in the order of Monday, Thursday, and Monday. [These fasts begin at dawn,] and it is permitted to eat and drink the preceding night. The Kohanim whose turn it is to serve in the *mishmar*[75] do not fast, because they are busy with the service.

On these days, all the people should assemble in the synagogue to pray and implore [God], as on all fasts.

---

[75] The kohanim who served in the Bais Hamikdash were divided into 24 families called mishmaros. Each family served one week during which time they were responsible for the Bais Hamikdash. Each mishmar was further divided into baatei av—heads of families and took turns doing the actual service each day.

3:3. If their prayers were not answered after these fasts, the *beis din* decrees another series of fasts on Monday, Thursday, and Monday. On these fasts, [which are more serious] we are only allowed to eat and drink until sunset [of the day before the fast] as we do on Yom Kippur.

The men serving in the *mishmar* should fast part of the day, though they do not fast the entire day. The men of the *beis av*— i.e., the members [of the *mishmar*] who are doing the service in the *Beis Hamikdash* on that day—should not fast at all.

On a fast such as these, when we must stop eating while it is still day, if a person has stopped eating, deciding not to eat any more that day, he may not change his mind and eat, even if there is still time during the day.

3:4. On these three fasts, one is forbidden to work during the day, though work is permitted during the [preceding] night. One may not to wash his entire body in hot water, but washing one's hands and feet is permitted. Because of this, the bathhouses are closed.

One may only anoint himself to remove filth. Marital relations are forbidden. Wearing shoes is forbidden in the city, but allowed when traveling. We pray in the synagogue and implore God as on all fasts.

Seven Additional Fasts

3:5. If their prayers were not answered after these fasts, the *beis din* decrees seven more communal fasts, starting on the next Monday, [followed by,] Thursday, Monday, Thursday, Monday, Thursday, and Monday.

On these seven fasts [as opposed to the earlier fasts] pregnant and nursing women are required to fast. On other fast days, although they are not required to fast, they should not treat themselves to delicacies. Instead, they should eat only what is necessary to nourish their babies.

3:6. On these seven fasts the men serving on the *mishmar* fast for the entire day. The men of the *beis av* fast part of the day, though not the entire day. All the prohibitions that apply to the second series of fasts also apply to these seven fasts.

3:7. These [seven] fasts are marked by additional features. We blow the trumpets, pray in the city square, appoint an elder to admonish the people and inspire them to do *teshuvah*, add six *berachos* in the morning and afternoon *Shemoneh esrei*, for a total of twenty-four *berachos*,[76] and close the stores.

On Mondays, towards evening [food] stores are open, however the door are only partially opened. On Thursdays [the stores] may be open the entire day [to allow people to buy food] in honor of Shabbos. A store with two entrances, can open one entrance [completely] and keeps the other closed. If the store has a display table or bench in front of it [which blocks the door], the door may be opened in the usual manner on a Thursday.

3:8. If their prayers were still not answered after these [seven] fasts, we cut down on business activities, on building luxury homes, [or wedding halls,] decorating ornate ceilings and walls, planting fancy plants like myrtle trees[77] and setting up tents [for gala celebrations].

We postpone betrothals and weddings, unless one has not fulfilled the mitzvah of "be fruitful and multiply."[78] One who has fulfilled this mitzvah is forbidden to have marital relations in a year of famine.

We tone down greetings, and Torah scholars do not exchange greetings at all. Rather, [they behave as people] who are shunned and banned by God. When greeted by an unlearned person, they return the greeting[79] in a low voice with a serious expression.

---

[76] The Rambam quotes the Mishnah which speaks of the time before the nineteenth *berachah* was added to the weekday *Shemoneh esrei*.

[77] But planting fruit trees is permitted.

[78] i.e., having a son and a daughter.

[79] So that the person should not feel offended.

3:9. The Torah scholars alone continue to fast, [starting the next] Monday, [and continuing the following] Thursday and Monday, until the end of the solar Nisan. However, the community need not [observe these additional fasts]. No more than these thirteen communal fasts are decreed because of drought.

When the [Torah scholars] fast until the end of Nisan, they are allowed to eat at night, do work, wash, anoint themselves, have marital relations, and wear shoes as on other fast days. They do not fast on *Rosh Chodesh* and Purim.

After Nisan, when the sun enters the zodiacal sign of Taurus, they should stop fasting. Since it did not rain from the beginning of the year, any rainfall at this point would be a sign of a curse.[80]

3:10. Where [do these rules] apply? In Eretz Yisrael and in countries with a similar [climate] as opposed to places where the rainy season begins before or after the seventeenth of Marcheshvan. [In those regions] if it does not rain in a timely manner, individuals should fast on Monday, Thursday, and Monday, excluding on Rosh Chodesh, Chanukah, or Purim.

Then they wait seven days. If it does not rain, the *beis din* decrees thirteen communal fasts, in the above-mentioned order.

3:11. On all communal fasts outside Eretz Yisrael it is permitted to eat during the night [until dawn], and the laws of the other fasts apply to them.[81] A communal fast like Yom Kippur is decreed only in Eretz Yisrael, and only because of a dry spell. This refers to the latter ten fasts, namely, the middle series of three fasts and the final series of seven fasts.

---

80 Since the rain would be of no benefit.
81 No prohibitions against work, washing, anointing oneself, marital relations, and wearing shoes.

The Fast Day Service

4:1. There is a special order of service on each day of the final seven fasts because of drought: The ark is taken to the city square, and all the people assemble wearing sackcloth. Wood ashes are placed on the ark and the *sefer Torah* to deepen the anguish and to humble the people's [hearts]. Someone places ashes on the heads of the *Nasi*[82] and the *Av Beis Din*,[83] where they wear *tefillin*. Thus they will be embarrassed and do *teshuvah*. Everyone else puts ashes on his own head.

4:2. One of the elder rabbis rises [to speak] while the people are seated. If there is no elder rabbi, a wise person is selected. If there is no wise person, a respected person is chosen.

He admonishes them [to do *teshuvah*], telling them: "Brothers, it is not sackcloth and fasting that will bring results, but rather *teshuvah* and good deeds. Indeed, regarding [the story of Yonah in] Nineveh it does not say about the people of Nineveh, 'And Hashem saw their sackcloth and their fasting,' but, '*Hashem saw their deeds*' (*Yonah* 3:10). And the Prophets tell us, '*Rend your hearts and not your garments*' (*Yoel* 2:13)." He continues preaching along these lines to the best of his ability until they humble themselves and return [to Hashem] in complete *teshuvah*.

4:3. After he finishes his sermon, the community rises to pray. A *chazzan* qualified to conduct the service on such fast days is chosen. If the one who gave the sermon is able to be the *chazzan* he should officiate; if not, someone else is chosen.

4:4. Who is qualified to be the *chazzan* at these fasts? One well-versed in the prayers, who regularly reads the Torah, the Prophets,

---

[82] Head of the Great Sanhedrin in Yerushalayim.
[83] Vice-President of the Great Sanhedrin and next in dignity to the *Nasi*.

and the Writings.[84] He should have children, be a poor man,[85] and work on a farm.[86]

None of his children, nor any member of his household, nor any close relative should be transgressors. Rather, his family should be free of sin; and he himself should have an unblemished reputation going back to his childhood.

He should be humble, well-liked by the community, and have a sweet and pleasant voice. If he is also an elderly person, so much the better. But even if he is not an elderly person, he is fit to be the *chazzan* if he has the other qualities.

4:5. The *chazzan* begins reciting the *Shemoneh esrei* until [before] the *berachah* of *Go'eil Yisrael*. He then recites [verses of] *Zichronos*[87] and *Shofaros*[88] that have to do with the distress [afflicting the people]. He also recites the psalms, "*In my distress I called to God, and He answered me*" (*Tehillim* 120) and "*I lift my eyes to the mountains; from where will my help come?* (*Tehillim* 121), "*Out of the depths I call You, O God*" (*Tehillim* 130), and "*A prayer of the afflicted, when he is faint*" (*Tehillim* 102).

4:6. He also inserts supplications [which he himself selects] to the best of his ability. He then says [the *berachah* of the *Shemoneh esrei*], "Please behold our affliction, take up our grievance, and speed our redemption," followed by supplications, and at the end of these he says, "He who answered Avraham, our Father at Mount Moriah will answer you and listen to your outcry today. Blessed are You, God, Redeemer of Yisrael."

4:7. He then adds a series of six *berachos*. In each he recites supplications and [relevant] verses from the Prophets and the Writings

---

84 And therefore will be able to supplicate properly as mentioned 4:7
85 So that his prayers come from the bottom of his heart.
86 Because he will have a personal interest that it should rain.
87 Verses that mention now Hashem remembers His people such as we say during Musaf of Rosh Hashana
88 Verses that mention the sounding of the Shofar as we say on Rosh Hashana.

with which he is familiar. Each of these *berachos* end with a specific phrase.

4:8. The first *berachah* ends with: "He who answered Moshe and our ancestors at the [parting of] the Red Sea will answer you and listen to your outcry today. Blessed are You, God, who remembers the forgotten."

4:9. The second *berachah* ends with: "He who answered Yehoshua at Gilgal[89] will answer you and listen to your outcry today. Blessed are You, God, who hears the sounding of the trumpets."

4:10. The third *berachah* ends with: "He who answered Shmuel at Mitzpah[90] will answer you and listen to your outcry today. Blessed are You, God, who hears an outcry."

4:11. The fourth *berachah* ends with: "He who answered Eliyahu at Mount Carmel[91] will answer you and listen to your outcry today. Blessed are You, God, who hears prayer."

4:12. The fifth *berachah* ends with: "He who answered Yonah in the belly of the fish will answer you and listen to your outcry today. Blessed are You, God, who answers in time of distress."

4:13. The sixth *berachah* ends with: "He who answered David and Shlomoh his son in Yerushalayim[92] will answer you and listen to your outcry today. Blessed are You, God, who has mercy on the land."

---

[89] Where Yehoshua prayed for victory over Jericho.

[90] Where Shmuel prayed that the Jews be saved from the Philistines (1 *Shmuel* 7:8-10).

[91] Where Eliyahu challenged the prophets of Baal and prayed that God should accept his offering (1 *Melachim* ch. 18).

[92] David prayed for the famine to end (2 *Shmuel* 21:1); Shlomoh prayed when he brought the Ark into the Holy of Holies (1 *Melachim* 8:22-53) (*Rashi, Taanis* 15a).

The people answer *Amen* after each of these *berachos*, just as we answer *Amen* after all *berachos*.

4:14. He continues with: "Heal us, God, then we will be healed," and he ends the *Shemoneh esrei* in its usual order, after which the trumpets are blown. This is the order of prayer [on these fasts] everywhere.

4:15. When this service was held in Yerushalayim [the people] gathered at the *Har Habayis* (Temple Mount), facing the East Gate praying according to the above order. When the *chazzan* reached the passage, "He who answered Avraham . . ." he would say, "Blessed are You Hashem, our God, the God of Yisrael for all eternity. Blessed are You Hashem, Redeemer of Yisrael." The people would respond, "Blessed is His name and the glory of His Kingdom for ever and ever."

The attendant then instructed the people who blow [the trumpets]: "Blow a *tekiah*[93], *kohanim*! Blow a *tekiah*!" The *chazzan* repeats, "He who answered Avraham our Father at Mount Moriah will answer you and listen to your outcry today." After this, the *kohanim* [blew the trumpets,] sounding *tekiah, teruah*[94], *tekiah*.

4:16. In the same way the *chazzan* ended the next *berachah*—the first of the six *berachos* saying—"Blessed are You, Hashem, our God, the God of Yisrael, for all eternity. Blessed are You, Hashem, who remembers the forgotten." [The people] responded, "Blessed be His name and the glory of His Kingdom for ever and ever."

The attendant then instructed those who blow [the trumpets]: "Blow a *teruah, kohanim*! Blow a *teruah*!" The *chazzan* repeated, "He who answered Moshe and our ancestors at the Red Sea, will answer you and listen to your outcry today." After this, the *kohanim* blew [the trumpets,] sounding *teruah, tekiah, teruah*.

---

93 tekiah—a long straight blast
94 teruah—a broken trumpet blast

4:17. For each [of these] *berachos*: the attendant either said "Blow a *tekiah!*," or "Blow a *teruah!*" until all seven *berachos* ended. Thus, sometimes the *kohanim* blew a series of *tekiah, teruah, tekiah*, and sometimes they blew a series of *teruah, tekiah, teruah* for a total of seven series.

This order was followed only on the *Har Habayis* (Temple Mount). When they blew *tekiah* and *teruah* sounds there, they blew the trumpets and the shofar together, as explained.[95]

4:18. Everywhere these fasts are decreed, all the people go to the cemetery after praying, to weep and offer supplications, as if to say, "If we don't repent of our sinful ways, we will die like the people [buried here]."

In all places on each of the communal fast days that are decreed because of adverse conditions, the *Ne'ilah* service is recited.

4:19. If [their prayers are answered,] and it begins to rain, how much rain must fall for the community to stop fasting? When the rain penetrates a handbreadth into parched earth, two handbreadths into ordinary earth, and three handbreadths into plowed earth.[96]

THE FOUR FASTS BECAUSE OF CALAMITIES

5:1. There are certain fast days observed by all of Israel commemorating [national] calamities that happened on those days. They are observed in order to arouse us to do *teshuvah*, reminding us of our wrongful conduct and the equally deplorable conduct of our ancestors which brought these disasters on them and on us. By reminding ourselves of these tragedies we will repent and improve [our conduct], as it says, "*They will confess their sin and the sin of their ancestors*" (*Vayikra* 26:40).

---

95 Chapter 1:4.
96 In all three cases the same amount of rain falls. Parched earth does not allow the rain to filter in easily, whereas the rain readily seeps into plowed earth.

5:2. These fast days are:

The Third of Tishrei. This is the day Gedaliah ben Achikam was slain and the ember of Yisrael that remained was extinguished, bringing their exile to completion.[97]

The Tenth of Teves. On this day, the wicked Nebuchadnezzar, King of Babylonia reached Yerushalayim and laid siege [to the city].

The Seventeenth of Tammuz. Five tragedies happened on this day:

1) The Tablets [of the Ten Commandments] were broken;

2) The offering of the daily sacrifice was suspended in the first *Beis Hamikdash*.

3) [The walls of] Yerushalayim were breached[98] leading to the destruction of the second *Beis Hamikdash*;

4) The wicked Apostomos burned a Torah scroll;[99]

5) He erected an idol in the *Beis Hamikdash*.

5:3. On *Tishah be'Av* (the Ninth of Av), five tragedies occurred:

1) It was decreed that the Jews in the desert would not enter *Eretz Yisrael*.[100]

2,3) The first and second *Beis Hamikdash* were destroyed.

4) The large city of Betar with a population of thousands of ten thousands was captured. They were ruled by a great king whom the entire Jewish people and the leading Sages thought to be the Messianic king. The city fell to the Roman legions and they were all slain in a catastrophe as disastrous as the destruction of the *Beis Hamikdash*.

---

[97] Gedaliah, the governor appointed by Nebuchadnezzar over the Jews remaining in Eretz Yisrael, was assassinated. Fearing the retaliation of the Babylonians, the Jews fled to Egypt, virtually draining Eretz Yisrael of Jews.

[98] When Titus and his army broke into the city.

[99] This event is mentioned in the Mishnah (*Taanis* 4:6). According to R. Bertinoro Apostomos was a Greek official during the second *Beis Hamikdash*.

[100] The spies Moshe sent to explore *Eretz Yisrael* returned, bringing back a slanderous report. Despondent, the Jews cried that night—the ninth of Av. As punishment Hashem decreed that the entire generation would die in the desert not entering Eretz Yisrael.

5) On that fateful day, the wicked Turnus Rufus (Tinneus Rufus) plowed the site of the Sanctuary and its surrounding area, thereby fulfilling the prophecy, "*Zion will be plowed like a field*" (*Michah* 3:12).

5:4. These four fasts are expressly mentioned by the Prophets: "*The fast in the fourth [month], the fast of the fifth [month] . . .* " (*Zechariah* 8:19). "*The fast of the fourth month*" refers to the Seventeenth of Tammuz, which is in the fourth month; "*the fast of the fifth month*" refers to *Tishah Be'Av* which is in the fifth month; "*The fast of the seventh month*" refers to the Third of Tishrei which is in the seventh month; "*the fast of the tenth month*" refers to the Tenth of Teves which is in the tenth month.

5:5. The custom of all Jews nowadays is to fast on the Thirteenth of Adar (*Taanis Esther*) also, in commemoration of the fasts that [the people] took upon themselves in the time of Haman, as it says, "*the obligation of the fasts with their lamentations*" (*Esther* 9:31).

If the Thirteenth of Adar falls on Shabbos, the fast is advanced to Thursday, the 11th of Adar. However, if any of the other fasts fall on Shabbos, the fast is postponed until after Shabbos. If these fasts fall on Friday, we fast on Friday.[101]

On all these fasts the trumpets are not blown, nor is the *Ne'ilah* service recited. However, the section of *Va'yechal* (*Shemos* 32:11) is read from the Torah, both in the *Shacharis* and *Minchah* services. On all these fasts, with the exception of *Tishah beAv*, we may eat and drink at night.[102]

5:6. When the month of Av arrives, we lessen our joy. During the week of *Tishah be'Av* it is forbidden to cut one's hair, do laundry,

---

[101] According to our fixed calendar only *Assarah beTeves* can fall on a Friday, but this rarely happens.

[102] Wearing shoes, washing, anointing oneself, and marital relations are also permitted on these fasts (*Shulchan Aruch, Orach Chayim* 550:2).

or wear a pressed garment—even one made of linen[103]—until after the fast. It is even forbidden to launder for use after the fast.

It is an accepted Jewish custom not to eat meat or take a bath during this week until after the fast.[104] In some places it is customary not to slaughter from *Rosh Chodesh Av* until after the fast.

5:7. All [the prohibitions of] *Tishah be'Av* apply at night as well as during the day. It is forbidden to eat during twilight, as on Yom Kippur.

One should not eat meat or drink wine at the meal before the fast.[105] However, one may drink grape juice within three days or less of its being pressed [since it has not fermented]. One may eat salted meat that was slaughtered more than three days earlier.[106] One should not eat two cooked dishes.[107]

5:8. When do [these restrictions] apply? When one eats [this meal] in the afternoon on the day before *Tishah be'Av*. However, if one eats a meal before noon, although this is the last meal he eats before the fast, he may eat whatever he wishes.

When the day before *Tishah be'Av* falls on Shabbos, one may eat and drink as much as he wishes, even serving a dinner as lavish as Shlomoh's banquet.

Similarly, when *Tishah be'Av* falls on Shabbos, there are no restrictions at all [on what may be eaten].

5:9. This is the way people who are unable to take too much [austerity] observe [the day before *Tishah be'Av*]. However, a devout

---

103 Linen clothes do not look as elegant after washing as other garments do.

104 The Ashkenazi custom is not to eat meat or drink wine during the Nine Days from *Rosh Chodesh Av* until after *Tishah be'Av*.

105 Even those who do not observe the custom of abstaining from meat and wine during the week of *Tishah be'Av* (or the Nine Days according to *minhag Ashkenaz*), should not partake of them during this meal.

106 According to the *Shulchan Aruch*, O.C. 552:2 it is our *minhag* to abstain even from these foods at this meal.

107 Because a meal consisting of two courses is an important meal which is out of place at this mournful time.

person of earlier generations sat alone by the stove. He ate dry bread and salt dipped in water and drank a pitcher of water in a worried, despondent frame of mind. He wept like a person [bemoaning] a dead relative lying before him.

Scholars should conduct themselves like this. We never ate a cooked dish, even lentils, on the day before *Tishah be'Av*, except [if it fell] on Shabbos.[108]

5:10. Pregnant women and nursing mothers must fast the whole day on *Tishah be'Av.*

[On *Tishah be'Av*] bathing [or washing] in either hot or cold water is forbidden; even dipping one's finger in water is forbidden. Anointing for pleasure, wearing shoes, and marital relation are also forbidden, as on Yom Kippur.

In places where it is customary to work, one may work. In places where it is customary not to work, one should not. Torah scholars should not do any work [regardless of the local custom]. Our Sages said, "One will not derive the slightest blessing from work done on [*Tishah be'Av*]."

5:11. Torah scholars do not greet each other on *Tishah be'Av.* Rather they grieve and sigh, like mourners. If a common person greets them, they answer in a low and gloomy tone of voice [so he should not feel slighted].

On *Tishah be'Av* it is forbidden to read from the Torah, the Prophets, or the Writings [or to study] Mishnah, Halachah, Talmud, or Aggadic books. One may only study *Iyov* (Job), *Eichah*, (Lamentations), and the prophecies of *Yirmeyah* foreboding evil. Children do not go to school.

---

108 Our *minhag* is to eat a regular meal before the *Minchah* service. Shortly before the fast, we sit on the ground or on a low stool. Only bread and a cold hard-boiled egg is eaten at this meal with a morsel of the bread dipped into ashes before being eaten.

There are some Torah scholars who do not wear *tefillin* on their head.[109]

COMMEMORATING THE DESTRUCTION OF THE *BEIS HAMIKDASH*

5:12. After the destruction of the *Beis Hamikdash*, the Sages of that generation ordained that no Jew build for himself a house painted and decorated in royal style. Instead, one should leave an unpainted space of a cubit square [as a reminder of the destruction of the *Beis Hamikdash*] opposite the entrance [so that it will be seen on entering]. If one buys a house with decorated walls, he may keep it as is; he need not remove the decorations.

5:13. Similarly, they ordained that a person who sets a table for guests[110] leave out one dish and one setting.

A woman should not wear all her jewelry, so she is not dressed to perfection.

We place ashes on the forehead of a bridegroom on the place where the *tefillin* are worn. All these practices were instituted to remember [the destruction of] Yerushalayim, as it says, "*If I forget you, O Yerushalayim, let my right hand forget its cunning, let my tongue stick to my palate if I cease to think of you, if I do not keep Yerushalayim in memory even at my happiest hour*" (*Tehillim* 137:5,6).

5:14. The Sages also decreed that no musical instruments be played for joy or listened to, [as a sign of mourning] for the destruction [of the *Beis Hamikdash*].[111] Even singing [without musi-

---

109 At the present time it is the custom in most communities not to wear *tefillin*—neither the head *tefillin* nor the arm *tefillin*, nor the *tallis*, in the *Shacharis* service.
110 Even a *se'udas mitzvah*, like a *bris* or a wedding, but at a Shabbos or Yom Tov meal nothing should be lacking (*Mishnah Berurah* 560:2 (5).
111 According to the *Rema* (*Orach Chaim* 560:3) "for the sake of a mitzvah, e.g., a wedding banquet, everything is permitted."

cal accompaniment] while drinking wine is forbidden, as it says, "*Do not drink wine with song*" (*Yeshayah* 24:9).

However, it has become the accepted Jewish custom to chant songs of praise and thanksgiving to God over wine.

5:15. Later on, they decreed that a bridegroom should not wear a crown or wreath, as it says, "*Remove the turban and lift off the crown*" (*Yechezkel* 21:31). They also decreed that a bride should not wear silver or gold crowns, though she may wear a garland of twisted cord.

5:16. On seeing the cities of Yehudah in ruin one recites, "*Your holy cities have become a desert,*" (*Yeshayah* 64:9), and rends his garments. On seeing Yerushalayim in ruin, one recites [the continuation of this verse,] "*Tzion has become a desert . . .*" On seeing the *Beis Hamikdash* in ruin, one recites, "*Our holy Beis Hamikdash, our pride . . . has been consumed by fire*" (ibid. 10) and rends his garments.

From which vantage point is one required to rend one's garments? From *Tzofim*. Afterwards, on reaching [the vicinity] of the *Beis Hamikdash* one rends them a second time. Arriving [in Yerushalayim] from the desert, if one saw the *Beis Hamikdash* first, he rends his garments because of the *Beis Hamikdash*, and deepens the tear because of Yerushalayim.

5:17. In all these cases, one rends his garments with his hands while standing. He rends all the garments he is wearing until he bares his chest. The tears are never mended though they may be stitched, hemmed, gathered, or sewn in a ladder pattern.

5:18. A person who visits Yerushalayim frequently is not required to rend his garments if he comes within thirty days of his last visit. If he comes after thirty days, he rends them.

5:19. All these fasts [of remembrance] will end when Mashiach comes. In fact, they will be transformed into *Yamim Tovim* and days of rejoicing and celebration, as it says, "*Thus said the Lord of Hosts: The fast of the fourth month, the fast of the fifth month, the fast of the seventh month, and the fast of the tenth month shall become occasions for joy and gladness, happy festivals for the House of Yehudah. And they shall love truth and peace*" (*Zechariah* 8:19).

HILCHOS MEGILLAH V'CHANUKAH
LAWS OF MEGILLAH AND CHANUKAH

READING THE MEGILLAH

1:1. It is a positive mitzvah, decreed by the Rabbis, to read the Megillah at the set time.[112] It is common knowledge that this mitzva was instituted by Prophets.[113] Everyone is required to read the Megillah: men, women, converts, and freed slaves. Even children should be trained to read it. Even *kohanim* interrupt their service [in the *Beis Hamikdash*] to hear the reading of the Megillah.

Similarly, Torah study is interrupted to hear the reading of the Megillah, and surely other mitzvos are set aside [to hear] the reading of the Megillah. Only [burying] a *meis mitzvah*—an [abandoned] corpse with no one to care for the burial—takes precedence to reading the Megillah. In such a case, one should bury the corpse first—reading the Megillah afterwards.

1:2. One can fulfill the mitzvah by reading the Megillah or by listening to it being read, provided that the one reading is obligated

---

[112] Since this mitzvah was ordained after the giving of the Torah, it is considered as given by the Rabbis.

[113] Chaggai, Zechariah, and Malachi who were members of the *Anshei Kensses Hagedolah* (the Men of the Great Assembly), the court convened by Ezra after the Jews returned to Eretz Yisrael from the Babylonian exile.

to hear the Megillah. One does not fulfill his obligation if he hears the reading from a minor or from a mentally deficient individual.

1:3. It is a mitzvah to read the entire Megillah both at night and during the day. The night reading may be done throughout the night and the day reading throughout the day.

Before the reading at night, one recites the following three *berachos*:

"Blessed are You, Hashem, our God, King of the universe, who has sanctified us with His commandments and has commanded us regarding the reading of the Megillah."

"Blessed are You, Hashem, our God, King of the universe, who has wrought miracles for our forefathers, in those days at this season."

"Blessed are You Hashem, our God, King of the universe, who has kept us alive, sustained us, and enabled us to reach this occasion."

One does not recite the last *berachah* before the day [reading]. In some places it is customary to recite the following *berachah* after the reading.

"Blessed are You, Hashem, our God, King of the universe, who takes up our grievance, judges our claim, avenges our wrong, exacts vengeance for us from our foes, and who brings just retribution on all the enemies of our soul. Blessed are You, Hashem, who exacts vengeance for His people Yisrael from all their foes, the God who brings salvation."

1:4. On what date should [the Megillah] be read?

The Sages fixed several dates for the reading of the Megillah, for it says, "*These days of Purim shall be observed at their proper times*" (*Esther* 9:31).

The Megillah is read on the following days.

The Megillah is read on the fifteenth of Adar in every city that was surrounded by a wall at the time of Yehoshua bin Nun whether in or out of Eretz Yisrael. This applies even if the city does not have a wall at the present time. Such a city is called a *k'rach*.

The Megillah is read on the fourteenth of Adar in every city not surrounded by a wall at the time of Yehoshua bin Nun. This applies even if the city is encircled by a wall at the present time. Such a city is called an *ir*.

1:5. In Shushan, the capital [of ancient Persia], the Megillah is read on the fifteenth [of Adar] although it was not surrounded by a wall at the time of Yehoshua bin Nun, because it was there that the miracle occurred [and at that time the Jews celebrated on the fifteenth of Adar], as it says, "*They rested on the fifteenth, and made it a day of feasting and merrymaking*" (*Esther* 9:18).

Why is the date of the Megilla reading linked to the time of Yehoshua bin Nun? In this manner, the commemoration of the Purim miracle includes a remembrance of Eretz Yisrael; the cities of Eretz Yisrael that were in ruin at the time of [the miracle], yet surrounded by a wall at the time of Yehoshua are honored by reading the Megillah at the same time it is read in Shushan.

SEUDAH, MISHLO'ACH MANOS, AND GIFTS TO THE NEEDY

2:12. The reader reads the names of Haman's ten sons and the word "ten" (*Esther* 9:7-10) that follows [this list], in one breath, indicating they were hanged and killed together.

It is a universally accepted custom for the reader [of the Megillah] to spread [and fold] the scroll like a letter as he reads it, in order to publicize the miracle. Upon conclusion, he rolls it up again, saying the [concluding] *berachah*.

2:13. It is forbidden to eulogize [the deceased] and to fast on both the fourteenth and fifteenth [of Adar]. [This prohibition] applies to everyone, wherever they may be, to inhabitants of the walled cities who celebrate only on the fifteenth and to inhabitants of unwalled cities who celebrate only on the fourteenth.

[In a leap year,] it is forbidden to eulogize and to fast on these two dates in the first Adar[114] as well as in the second Adar. When residents of villages read the Megillah earlier, either on the Monday or Thursday before Purim,[115] they are permitted to eulogize and to fast on the day they read the Megillah but they are forbidden to eulogize and fast on the fourteenth and the fifteenth of Adar, even though they do not read the Megillah.

2:14. It is a mitzvah for residents of villages and unwalled cities to consider the fourteenth of Adar—and for residents of walled cities to consider the fifteenth of Adar—a day of gladness and feasting, and sending food to their friends and gifts to the poor.

Although it is permitted to work on [these days], our Sages frowned upon it saying: Whoever works on Purim will never derive any benefit from it.

If villagers read the Megillah earlier—on Monday or Thursday—and give gifts to the poor on that day, they have fulfilled their obligation. However, the rejoicing and feasting [of Purim and *mishlo'ach manos*] may be done only on the fourteenth day. If one performs these mitzvos earlier, he has not fulfilled his obligation. Likewise, one who eats the Purim feast on the night [of Purim] does not fulfill his obligation.

2:15. What should be served at this feast? One should eat meat, preparing a meal as lavish as he can afford. He should drink wine until he becomes drunk and falls asleep.

One must also send either two portions of meat, two other cooked dishes, or two other food items to a friend, as it says, "*sending food to their friends*" (*Esther* 9:22), meaning, two portions to one friend. The more [friends] one sends food gifts to, the more praiseworthy he is. If one cannot afford it, he should exchange his

---

[114] Although Purim is celebrated in the second Adar. According to the Rema (697:1) fasting and eulogies are permitted, but *Tachanun* should be omitted.

[115] Since on Monday and Thursday they travel to nearby cities, the Sages did not want to burden them to make an additional trip to hear the Megillah.

meal [with a friend], thereby fulfilling [the mitzvah of] sending food to one's friend.

2:16. One is required to give [charity] to the poor on the day of Purim. At the very least one should give one gift each to two poor persons—be it money, cooked dishes, or other foods, as it says, "*gifts to the poor*" meaning, two gifts to two poor people.[116]

We are not particular when handing out Purim gifts [to the poor]. Whoever puts out his hand to beg, should be given alms. Money given [to a charity fund] to be distributed on Purim should not be used for other *tzedakah* purposes.

2:17. It is better to give charity to the poor than to prepare a lavish feast or send *mishlo'ach manos* to one's friends. There is no greater joy and no more glorious deed than gladdening the hearts of the poor, the orphan, the widow, and the convert. He who gladdens the hearts of these unfortunates is likened to the Divine Presence, about Whom it says "*Reviving the spirits of the lowly, reviving the hearts of the contrite*" (*Yeshayah* 57:15).

2:18. The books of the Prophets and the Writings will be rescinded in the era of Mashiach, with the exception of the Book of Esther. It will remain intact, as will the five books of the Torah and the *halachahs* of the Oral law, which will never be repealed.

Although all memories of the persecutions [inflicted on the Jewish people] will be forgotten, as it says, "*The former troubles will be forgotten, will be hidden from My eyes*" (*Yeshayah* 65:16), the celebration of Purim will not be revoked, as it says, "*These days of Purim will never stop being celebrated by the Jews, and their memory will never leave their children*" (*Esther* 9:28).

---

[116] *matanos*, "gifts" and *evyonim*, "poor persons" are in the plural.

LAWS OF CHANUKAH
Historical Background

3:1. During the period of the Second Beis Hamikdash, the Greeks rulers issued drastic decrees against the Jewish people, forbidding them to study Torah or do mitzvos, in order to destroy their religion. They robbed them of their property, violated their daughters, and entered the Beis Hamikdash, desecrating and defiling its sanctity. Their cruel oppression brought great hardship to the Jews, until the God of our fathers took pity on them and saved them from their hands. The sons of the Hasmonean High Priest defeated and slew them and saved the Jewish people from their tyranny. The kingdom of Israel was reestablished under the rule of one of the *kohanim* and lasted for more than two hundred years, until the destruction of the Second Temple.

3:2. The Jews prevailed over their enemies, on the twenty-fifth of Kislev. When they entered the Beis Hamikdash, they found only a single cruse of pure olive oil. This oil was sufficient for only one day, yet they were able to light the Menorah with it for eight days until they could pound olives and extract pure oil.

3:3. For this reason, the Sages of that generation decreed that the eight days beginning on the twenty-fifth of Kislev, should be set aside as days of rejoicing and praising [God]. Toward evening during these eight days, lights are lit at the entrance of the houses to proclaim the miracle. These days are called Chanukah. Like Purim, fasting and giving funeral orations are forbidden on Chanukah. Lighting the candles on Chanukah is a Rabbinic mitzvah, as is the reading of the Megillah [on Purim].

The Mitzvah of Kindling the Menorah

3:4. Whoever is required to read the Megillah is also obligated to kindle the Chanukah lights. On the first night, a person lighting [the Menorah] recites the following three *berachos*:

"Blessed are You, Hashem, our God, King of the universe, who has sanctified us with His commandments, and has commanded us to kindle the Chanukah light."

"Blessed are You, Hashem, our God, King of the universe, who has wrought miracles for our forefathers, in those days at this season."

"Blessed are You Hashem, our God, King of the universe, who has kept us alive, sustained us, and enabled us to reach this occasion."

One who did not recite a *berachah* [over his own Chanukah lights], should recite the last two *berachos*: *She'asa nissim* and *Shehecheyanu* upon seeing a Menorah. On the other nights, one who lights the Menorah should recite two *berachos*: [*Lehadlik ner* and *She'asa nissim*], while one who sees the Menorah should recite one beracha [*She'asa nissim*]; the *berachah* of *Shehecheyanu* is recited only on the first night.

3:5. On each of these eight days the entire *Hallel*[117] *is recited*. Before saying *Hallel*, one should say the *berachah*" . . . who has sanctifies us with His commandments and commanded us, to complete the *Hallel*."[118] This applies whether the *Hallel* is said by an individual or by a congregation.

Although the reading of the *Hallel* is a mitzvah decreed by the Sages, we recite the *berachah* [stating] "who has sanctified us with His commandments and commanded us," just as we do with the mitzva of reading of the Megillah and making an *eiruv* [which are also rabbinically ordained].[119]

---

117 *Tehillim* 113-118.

118 Our *minhag* is to say, "to read the *Hallel*"

119 The wording of the *berachah* suggests that the mitzvah was given by Hashem, although these mitzvos are Rabbinical decrees. However, in a sense, all Rabbinical mitzvos were ordained by the Torah, for the Torah commands us to obey the rulings of the Sages. Thus, by observing the mitzvos of the Sages we are doing Hashem's will.

On the other hand, if the Sages instituted an obligation because of a doubt—for example, the tithing of *demai*[120]—a *berachah* is not said. [In light of this one may ask:] Why do we say a *berachah* over the second day of Yom Tov; after all, the Rabbis instituted its observance only because of doubt?[121] [However a *berachah* is said in this case,] because people might otherwise treat [the second day Yom Tov] with disdain.

RECITING THE *HALLEL*

3:6. The recitation of *Hallel* is a Rabbinic ordinance, not only on Chanukah, but on all occasions when we recite the complete *Hallel*.

On eighteen days in the year it is a mitzvah to recite the entire *Hallel*, namely:

the eight days of Sukkos,

the eight days of Chanukah,

the first day of Pesach,

the day of Shavuos.

Hallel is not recited on Rosh Hashanah and Yom Kippur since they are days of repentance, awe, and fear, not days of exuberance. *Hallel* is not said on Purim, because the Sages decreed that reading the Megillah takes the place of *Hallel*.

3:7. In places where the Yamim Tovim are celebrated for two days, *Hallel* is recited on 21 days:

the nine days of Sukkos,

the eight days of Chanukah,

---

120 *Demai* refers to the produce of an unlearned farmer, who may not have separated the tithes. The Sages ruled that a person buying such produce must separate the tithes because of the doubt attached to it.

121 When *Rosh Chodesh* was determined on the basis of visual sighting of the new moon, people in distant regions that could not be reached by the court's messengers were in doubt on what day Yom Tov should be observed. Therefore they observed two days Yom Tov. See Hilchos Kiddush Hachodesh, ch. 5.

the [first] two days of Pesach,
the two days of Shavuos.

[Unlike the recitation of *Hallel* on Yom Tov, which is rabbinically ordained,] *Hallel* on Rosh Chodesh is a custom and not a mitzvah.[122] It is said only in a congregation [of ten adult males]. [Since it is only a custom] two paragraphs are omitted. We do not recite it with a *berachah*, since a *berachah* is not recited over a *minhag*. A person praying alone should not say the *Hallel* at all [on Rosh Chodesh].[123] However, if he began to say *Hallel*, he should complete it, omitting the paragraphs the congregation omits.

So too, on the last six days of Pesach, *Hallel* is said, skipping those paragraphs.

3:8. Which paragraphs are skipped?

We recite from the beginning of *Hallel* until the words *chalamish lema'yeno mayim*. We then skip and begin with *Hashem zecharanu yevareich*, until *halleluyah*. We then skip and begin saying *Mah ashiv laShem*, continuing until *halleluyah*. We then skip and begin saying *Min hameitzar karasi*, continuing until the end of *Hallel*. This is the commonly accepted custom. Others omit different passages.[124]

3:9. *Hallel* may be recited throughout the entire day. A person who reads *Hallel* out of sequence does not fulfill his obligation. If a person reads part of *Hallel*, pauses, then resumes reading and pauses again, even if he pauses long enough to complete the entire *Hallel*, he fulfills his obligation.

On the days when the entire *Hallel* is recited, one may interrupt between the chapters, but not within a chapter. On the days when the shortened version of *Hallel* is said, one may interrupt even within a chapter.

---

[122] Since doing work is not forbidden on Rosh Chodesh, there is no requirement to say *Hallel* (*Arachin* 10b).

[123] Our custom is that even a person praying alone should say the *Hallel* with a *berachah* (see *Rema* and *Mishnah Berurah* on *Orach Chaim* 422:2).

[124] Both the Ashkenazi and Sephardi communities have the *minhag* of skipping the portions *Lo lanu* (*Tehillim* 115:1-11) and *Ahavti* (*Tehillim* 116:1-11). We then continue with *Mah ashiv* until the end of *Hallel*.

3:10. Whenever the complete *Hallel* is said, one recites a *berachah* before *Hallel*. In places where it is customary to say a *berachah* afterwards, a *berachah* should be said.[125]

What is the text of this *berachah*?

"All Your works shall praise You, Hashem, our God. And the righteous and devout ones who carry out Your will, and Your nation, the House of Yisrael, will joyously praise Your name. For it is good to praise You, O God, and it is fitting to sing praises to Your name. From this world to the World to Come, You are the Almighty. Blessed are You, Hashem, the King who is glorified, praised, and extolled, who is living and enduring. He shall constantly reign over us for all eternity."

Various *Minhagim*

3:11. In some places it is customary to repeat each verse from *Odecha ki anisani* (*Tehillim* 118:2) until the end of *Hallel*.[126] In places where this is the custom, the verses should be repeated, otherwise they should not be repeated.[127]

3:12. In the days of the Talmud, the Sages said the *Hallel* the following way:[128] After reciting the *berachah*, the *chazzan* began the *Hallel* saying, *Halleuyah*, and the congregation responded *Halleluyah*.

[The *chazzan*] then read, "*Hallelu avdei Hashem*, with the congregation responding, *Halleluyah*. He then read, *Halleu es shem Hashem*, and the congregation responded, *Halleluyah* once again. He continued, *Yehi shem Hashem mevorach mei'atah ve'ad olam*, with the congregation responding, *Halleluyah*.

---

125 Nowadays, it is the universal *minhag* to say this berachah.

126 Rashi in *Sukkah* 38a explains that the reason is to conform with the previous verses which restate the same idea with different words, for example: *Hashem's hand is raised triumphantly; Hashem's right hand does valiantly.*"

127 Our *minhag* is to repeat these verses.

128 As described in *Sukkah* 38b.

After every line [of the *Hallel* the congregation responded, *Halleluyah*], for a total of 123 times. This number can be remembered easily because it is the same as the years of Aharon's life.

3:13. When the *chazzan* began a new chapter, the congregation repeated the first line he recited. For example, when he chanted the line, *Betzeis Yisrael miMitzrayim,* the congregation repeated it.[129] The *chazzan* then continued with, *Beis Yaakov me'am lo'ez,* and the congregation responded, *Halleluyah.* [They continued to respond *Halleluyah* after each line] until the *chazzan* chanted *Ahavti ki yishma Hashem es koli,* which is the beginning of the next chapter and the congregation repeated it. And when the *chazzan* chanted, *Hallelu es Hashem kol goyim,* the congregation repeated that phrase.

3:14. When the *chazzan* chanted, *Ana Hashem hoshiah na,* the congregation repeated this line, although it is not the beginning of a chapter. The same was true of, *Ana Hashem hatzlichah na.* When he chanted, *Baruch haba,* the congregation responded *Beshaim Hashem.*

If the *chazzan* was a minor, a slave, or a woman, the congregation repeated the entire *Hallel,* word by word after the *chazzan* [instead of responding to the phrases chanted by the *chazzan*].

This was the original custom, and it should be kept up. But I have seen in many places different customs in the recitation of the Hallel and the response of the congregation.

The Order of Precedence

4:12. The mitzvah of kindling Chanukah lights should be treasured. One should be careful to observe it, thus publicizing the miracle and intensifying our praise of God and our thanks for the

---

129 Nowadays, most communities do not follow this *minhag.*

miracles He performed for us. One who lives off charity, should borrow money or sell his garment to buy oil and lamps for kindling.

4:13. If one has only a single *perutah*[130], he should use his coin to buy oil [for the Menorah] rather than wine for *Kiddush* of Shabbos Chanukah. Since both these mitzvos are decreed by the Rabbis, it is preferable to light the Menorah, since it commemorates the miracle.

4:14. If one [can only afford to] either kindle the [Shabbos] lights in his home or light the Menorah, or [in a different situation,] buy [either oil for] the [Shabbos] lights in his home or [wine] for *Kiddush*, kindling the [Shabbos] lights for the home takes precedence, because the [Shabbos] lights promote domestic peace [for the light helps people see and avoid stumbling in the dark.]

[Domestic peace is of overriding importance]; for the Torah decrees that God's name be blotted out to create peace between husband and wife.[131]

Peace is wonderful, for the entire Torah was given to bring about peace in the world, as it says, *"Her ways are pleasant ways, and all her paths are peaceful"* (*Mishlei* 3:17).

---

[130] a small coin

[131] A *sotah*, a wife suspected of adultery, was tested through a scroll containing a curse against her in which God's name was written. This scroll was erased in water, and the writing including God's name was dissolved. The water was given to the *sotah* to drink. If she was innocent, the water did not harm her, and the husband's suspicions were laid to rest, and domestic peace was reestablished (*Bamidbar* 5:11-31).

MISHNE TORAH - YAD HACHZAKAH

ספר נשים וקדושה

THE BOOK OF WOMEN

Laws of Marriage

Laws of Divorce

Laws of *Yibbum* and *Chalitzah*

Laws Concerning Forbidden Relations

HILCHOS ISHUS
Laws of Marriage

———◈———

Consecration and Betrothal

1:1. Before the Torah was given, if a man met a woman in the street, and they mutually agreed to get married, he made her his wife by bringing her to his home and having marital relations with her. When the Torah was given, Jewish men were commanded that before one marries a woman, he must [formally] acquire her in the presence of witnesses. Afterward she can become his wife. For it says, *"When a man acquires a woman and has relations with her"* (*Devarim* 22:13), [implying, that he must acquire her before having relations with her].

1:2. Marrying a woman [by formally acquiring her as a wife] is a positive mitzvah of the Torah.

There are three ways to acquire a wife: handing over money to her, giving her a marriage contract, or through marital relations.

[Acquisition through] marital relations or through a marriage contract are based on Torah law, whereas [acquisition through] money was instituted by the Rabbis. These ways of acquiring [a wife] are universally referred to as *kiddushin*—consecration, or *eirusin*—betrothal. A woman, acquired in any of these three ways, is referred to as consecrated or betrothed.

1:3. Once a woman has been formally acquired she has the status of being consecrated, and is considered married, though she has not had marital relations nor entered her husband's home. Should anyone other than her husband have relations with her, he is liable to the death penalty imposed by the court. If her husband wants to divorce her, he must give her a *get*—a bill of divorce.

1:4. Before the Torah was given, if a man met a woman in the street, and they mutually agreed, he could pay her, have relations, and then move on. Such a woman is referred to as a *kedeishah*—a harlot.

When the Torah was given, [relations with] a harlot became forbidden, as it says, *"There shall not be a harlot among the daughters of Israel"* (*Devarim* 23:18). Therefore, one who has relations with a woman to satisfy his lust, without *kiddushin*, receives lashes as prescribed by the Torah, because she is considered a harlot.

KIDDUSHIN—CONSECRATION OF THE MARRIAGE

3:1. How does a man marry a woman through the *kiddushin* ceremony?

If he marries her by giving her money, he must give her a *perutah*[1] or an article worth no less than a *perutah*.

[Before handing it to her,] he says to her, "You are consecrated to me . . . ," or, "You are betrothed to me . . .," or, "You become my wife through this." He must give her [the money or the article] in front of witnesses.

The man makes this declaration signifying that he is acquiring the woman as his wife, and it is he who gives her the money.

---

[1] a small coin.

TRADITIONAL *KIDDUSHIN*

3:21. Although [marital relations] is the primary method of acquiring a wife, it has become a long-standing Jewish custom to consecrate [a woman] by handing her money. If one wishes to consecrate [a woman] by giving her a marriage contract, he may do so, but one may not consecrate a woman through marital relations.

If a man did consecrate [a woman] through marital relations, he receives lashes for rebelliousness,[2] because the Jewish people should not act shamelessly in this regard. Nevertheless, the *kiddushin* is valid.

3:22. Similarly, a man who consecrates a woman without a prior engagement, or a man who [casually] consecrates a woman in the street, is given lashes for rebelliousness, although the *kiddushin* are valid. [This was enacted] to avoid a climate of immorality; and in order that [the woman] should not appear as a harlot as was accepted before the giving of the Torah.

3:23. When a man consecrates a woman, through himself or an agent, he[3] or his agent recites a *berachah* before the consecration, just as a *berachah* is recited before one performs any mitzvah.

[After reciting the *berachah*,] he consecrates the woman. If he consecrated the woman without saying the *berachah*, he does not say the *berachah* afterward; it would be a pointless once the act has been done.

3:24. What is the text of the *berachah*?
"Blessed are You Hashem, our God, King of the universe, who has sanctified us with His commandments, and has separated us from forbidden unions; who forbade betrothed women to us, and per-

---

2   which is the punishment given for violating Rabbinic decrees.
3   It is the universal custom today that the rabbi conducting the wedding ceremony recites the *berachah*, so as not to embarrass a groom who is unable to say the *berachah*.

mitted women who are married to us through *chuppah* (canopy) and *kiddushin*. Blessed are You, Hashem, who sanctifies Yisrael." This is the *berachah* of *eirusin*—betrothal.

The people have instituted the custom of reciting this *berachah* over wine or beer. If wine is available, one says the *berachah* over wine first, the *berachah* of *eirusin* afterwards, and then consecrates the woman.[4] If wine or beer are not available, one only says [the *berachah* of *eirusin*].

MARRIAGE WITH A PRECONDITION

8:4. If a man says to a woman, "Behold, you are consecrated to me, on condition that I know how to read," he must know how to read from the Torah, translating the text according to the translation of Onkelos the convert.

If he says to her, ". . . on condition that I am a reader," he must know how to read the Torah, the *Nevi'im* (Books of the Prophets) and the *Kesuvim* (Writings), with the correct grammatical pronunciation.

[If he tells her,] ". . . on condition that I know how to study the Mishnah," he must know how to read the Mishnah. ". . . on condition that I am a sage of the Mishnah," he must know how to read the Mishnah, the *Sifra*,[5] the *Sifrei*,[6] and the *Tosefta* of Rabbi Chiya.[7]

8:5. [If he tells her,] ". . . on condition that I am a student [of the Torah]," he need not be a student of ben Azzai and ben Zoma's

---

4   Our custom is for the *mesader kiddushin* to say the *berachah* over the wine, and then the *berachah* of *eirusin*. The *chasan* and the *kallah* drink from the wine, after which the *chasan* consecrates the *kallah*.

5   a halachic Midrash on *Vayikra*, composed by Rav, the leader of the first generation of Amoraim in Babylonia.

6   a halachic Midrash on *Bamidbar* and *Devarim*, composed by Rav.

7   a collection of oral laws that were not included by Rabbi Yehudah HaNasi in the Mishnah.

stature.[8] Rather, he should be able to answer questions about his studies. [This includes] even the simple laws of the Yamim Tovim that are taught in public as Yom Tov approaches, to familiarize the people with them.

[If he tells her,] ". . . provided I am a wise man," he need not be as wise as Rabbi Akiva and his colleagues. Rather, he should be able to offer a wise insight on any subject when asked.

". . . provided I am robust," he need not be like Avner ben Ner[9] or Yo'av[10] Rather, his friends should be intimidated by his strength.

". . . on condition that I am rich," he need not be as wealthy as Rabbi Elazar ben Azariah.[11] It is enough if the people of his city honor him because of his wealth.

". . . on condition that I am a *tzaddik*," even if he is known to be a complete evildoer, the woman is consecrated, because it is possible he was considering *teshuvah* at that moment [which makes him a *tzaddik*, since all his sins are forgiven].

". . . provided that I am wicked," even if he is known to be a perfect *tzaddik*, the woman is consecrated, because it is possible he was thinking of idolatry at that moment. The sin of idol worship is so grave that one who merely thinks of serving [idols, without actually worshipping them] is considered wicked. For it says, [regarding the sin of idol worship] *"Take care that your heart not be tempted"* (*Devarim* 11:16) [implying that the thought of idol worship alone is sinful]. And it says, *"Thus I will hold the House of Yisrael to account for their thoughts [because they have all been estranged from Me through their idols]"* (*Yechezkel* 14:5).

---

8   brilliant disciples of Rabbi Akiva. They met a tragic fate when they "gazed toward the *Shechinah*," exploring the mysteries of the spiritual world, as told in *Chagigah* 14b.

9   the commander of King Shaul's army.

10   the commander of King David's forces.

11   who used to give 12,000 calves as the tithe of his herd (*Shabbos* 54b).

EIRUSIN AND NISUIN

10:1. The Rabbis decreed that a woman [though] consecrated through the *eirusin* ceremony is forbidden to have marital relations with her husband as long as she is living in her father's house.[12] A man who has marital relations with his betrothed [before she becomes his wife through *nisuin*] while she is still in her father's house receives "lashes for rebelliousness."

Even when one consecrates [his wife] through marital relations,[13] he is forbidden to have relations with her again until he brings her to his home and withdraws into a private room with her [for *yichud*], thereby setting her apart as his wife.

The seclusion of husband and wife in a private room is called "entering into the *chuppah*" and it is universally referred to as *nisuin*.[14]

When a man has relations with his *arusah* after the betrothal, with intent to perform *nisuin*, she becomes his wife at the beginning of marital relations. This makes her his wife in all aspects.[15]

SHEVA BERACHOS

10:3. The marriage *berachos* must be recited in the *chasan*'s house before the *nisuin* takes place.[16]

---

[12] It should be remembered that the wedding ceremony consists of two separate stages. The first is *kiddushin*, also called *eirusin* (betrothal). When the *eirusin* is accomplished the couple is considered as married to the extent that their relationship can be severed only through divorce or death. However the couple may not live together until the next stage which is called *nisuin*. In Talmudic times the ceremonies of *eirusin* and *nisuin* took place at different times, whereas nowadays *nisuin* follows immediately after *erusin*. The present *Halachah* deals with the *kiddushin* or *eirusin* phase of the marriage, before the *nisuin* has taken place.

[13] Having marital relations is one of the three ways of acquiring a wife (see 1:2).

[14] After the ceremony under the *chuppah* (canopy) the couple withdraws to a private room, called *yichud* room.

[15] All the rights and obligations specified in the *kesubah* apply.

[16] This applies when the wedding was held in the chasan's house. In other words, the *berachos* should be said under the *chuppah*, before the couple leave for the *yichud* room.

The following six *berachos* are recited:

"Blessed are You Hashem, our God, King of the universe, who has created everything for His glory."

"Blessed are You Hashem, our God, King of the universe, who fashioned the Man."

"Blessed are You Hashem, our God, King of the universe, who fashioned man in His image, in the image of His likeness and prepared for Him—from Himself—a building for eternity. Blessed are You Hashem, who fashioned the Man."

"Bring intense joy and exultation to the barren one [*Yerushalayim*] through the ingathering of her children in her midst in gladness. Blessed are You, Hashem, who gladdens Tzion through her children."

"Gladden the beloved companions as You gladdened Your creation in the *Gan Eden* of primeval time. Blessed are You Hashem, who gladdens groom and bride."

"Blessed are You, Hashem, our God, King of the universe. who created joy and gladness, groom and bride, mirth, glad song, pleasure, delight, love, brotherhood, and companionship. Hashem, our God, let there soon be heard in the cities of Yehudah and the streets of Yerushalayim the sound of joy and the sound of gladness, the voice of the groom and the voice of the bride, the sound of the grooms' jubiliance from their canopies and of youths from their song-filled feasts. Blessed are You, who gladdens the groom with the bride."

10:4. If wine is available, a *berachah* over the cup of wine is recited first. Afterwards, the above *berachos* are said over the cup of wine, for a total of seven *berachos*.

In some places a myrtle branch is brought together with the wine. The *berachah* over the myrtle is said after the *berachah* over the wine, and then the six *berachos* mentioned above are recited.

10:5. The *sheva berachos* are said only in the presence of a *minyan*. The *chasan* is counted as part of the *minyan*.

10:12. Our Sages decreed that one who marries a virgin celebrates with her for seven days, neither going to work nor doing business. Rather he should eat, drink, and rejoice. [He celebrates for seven days,] regardless of whether he has been married before. Our sages decreed that one who marries a non-virgin celebrates for three days whether or not he has been married before.

The Husband's Rights and Obligations

12:1. When a man marries a woman, whether she is a virgin or not, whether she is above the age of majority or a minor, and whether she is Jewish from birth, a convert, or a freed slave, he assumes ten obligations and is entitled to four rights.

12:2. Three of the ten obligations are Torah law, namely: *she'eirah, kesusah,* and *onasah* (*Shemos* 21:10).

She'eirah means he must provide her sustenance; *kesusah* means he must give her clothing, and *onasah* refers to her conjugal rights.

The seven duties of a husband decreed by the Rabbis are terms [of the marriage contract] set by the court. The first is the basic requirement of the marriage contract itself[17]. The other [six] are referred to as "terms of the *kesubah*", namely:

1) to provide medical treatment if she becomes sick;

2) to redeem her if she is taken captive;

3) to bury her if she dies;

4) the right for her to continue living in his home after his death as long as she remains a widow;

5) the right for her daughters to be supported from his estate after his death until they are betrothed;

6) the right for her sons to inherit her *kesubah* in addition to their share of her husband's estate together with their brothers [born to their father's other wives, if she dies prior to her husband's death].

---

[17] To pay her a set sum of money if he dies or divorces her.

12:3. The four rights the husband is entitled to are all ordained by the Rabbis, namely:

1) the right to any income she earns from her work;

2) the right to any ownerless object she finds;

3) the right to benefit from the profits of her property during her lifetime;

4) the right to inherit her property if she dies during his lifetime. His rights to her property take precedence over [the claims of] all others.

12:4. Our Sages also decreed that a [husband's right to the] income of his wife's work should match the sustenance [she receives from her husband]; that [the husband's obligation to redeem her] should match [his right to] the income from her property; and that the obligation to bury her should match [the right to] inherit the property mentioned in her *kesubah*.

In light of that, a wife has the right to say, "I do not demand that you provide for my sustenance, but I will not work for you," and she cannot be forced to work. However, a husband does not have the prerogative to say, "I will not provide for your sustenance, and I will do without the income of your work," since the wife's income may not be enough to sustain herself. Because of this condition, [the husband's duty to provide for his wife's] sustenance is considered to be one of the terms of the *kesubah*.

Providing Sustenance for Children

12:14. A man is required to provide food for his children, both boys and girls, until they are six years old just as he is required to provide food for his wife.

Afterwards, he continues to support them until they reach majority, as decreed by the Rabbis. If he refuses, he is reprimanded and publicly shamed, and urged [to change his ways]. If he still refuses to support them, a public announcement is made about him,

"So-and-so is heartless. He refuses to provide food for his children. He is worse than an impure bird which feeds its chicks." Nevertheless, he should not be forced to provide sustenance for children six years and older.

12:15. To whom is this law referring? It refers to a person who is not known to be well off, and it is not known whether or not he is required to give *tzedakah*, However, if he is well-to-do with the wherewithal to give enough *tzedakah* to provide for his children's needs, his property is confiscated against his will and turned over to charity; thus his children's needs are taken care of until they reach majority.

THE MITZVAH TO HAVE CHILDREN

15:1. A woman is allowed to forgo her conjugal rights. When does this apply? When her husband has children and thus fulfilled the mitzvah to procreate. However, if he has not fulfilled this mitzvah, he is required to have marital relations until he fathers children. For this is a positive mitzvah of the Torah, as it says, "*Be fertile and increase*" (*Bereishis* 1:28) [and a woman may not keep her husband from fulfilling his obligation].

15:2. The mitzvah of having children is binding on a man, not on his wife.

When does a man become obligated to fulfill this mitzvah? When he becomes seventeen years old.[18] If he reaches the age of twenty and has not married, he is transgressing by not fulfilling this positive mitzvah.

However, if he is fully immersed in Torah learning, and is reluctant to marry because working to support his wife would prevent him from learning Torah, he is allowed to postpone [marriage]; for a person busy doing a mitzvah is free from the obligation of doing

---

[18] The Rambam interprets the Mishnah in *Avos* 5:2, which says that an eighteen-year old should go to the *chuppah*, to mean : in the eighteenth year of his life.

another mitzvah. Surely the mitzvah of learning Torah [exempts one from the obligation of marriage].

15:3. When a person longs to learn Torah all the time, so that he is consumed with its study like ben Azzai,[19] who did not marry because he was engrossed in Torah every waking moment, he is not considered a transgressor.

This holds true, provided his passion does not overpower him. However, if his natural impulse gets the better of him, he is obligated to marry, even if he is already a father, so he should not be aroused by sinful thoughts.

15:4. How many children must a man father to fulfill this mitzvah? One boy and one girl, for it says, "*He created them male and female*" (*Bereishis* 5:2). If the son is impotent, or if the daughter is barren, he has not fulfilled the mitzvah.

15:5. A man has fulfilled the mitzvah of "*be fertile and increase*" even if his children die, if they left behind children of their own, since grandchildren are considered children.

When does this apply? When one's grandchildren are both male and female, the offspring of a male and a female, even if the grandson is the son of his daughter and the granddaughter is the daughter of his son. Since they are the offspring of two of his children, he has fulfilled the mitzvah of "*be fertile and increase*." However, if he had a son and a daughter who both died, and [one did not leave any children, whereas] the other left a son and a daughter, the grandfather has not fulfilled this mitzvah.

15:16. Even if a man has fulfilled the mitzvah of "*be fertile and increase*," he is still required by Rabbinic ordinance to continue fathering children as long as he is physically able to do so. For he who adds a soul to the Jewish people is considered as if he built an entire world.

---

[19] See *Yevamos* 63b.

Similarly, it is a Rabbinic mitzvah for a man to live with a wife, to avoid being aroused by sinful thoughts. Similarly, a woman should live with a husband, so she will not be suspected [of immorality].

15:19. Our Sages commanded a man to honor his wife more than he honors himself and love her as he loves himself. If he is wealthy, he should shower her with favors according to his means. Rather than intimidating her, he should speak gently, never using a sad or angry tone of voice.

16:20. Similarly, the Sages commanded a woman to honor her husband greatly and respect him, carrying out his instructions, as if he were an officer or a king. She should follow his wishes distancing herself from the things he dislikes.

This is the way holy and pure Jewish men and women conduct themselves to create a beautiful and admirable marriage.

HILCHOS GERUSHIN

LAWS OF DIVORCE

TEN PRINCIPLES

1:1. A woman may be divorced only by receiving a written document called a *get*.

The Torah sets forth ten basic principles for dissolving a marriage. They are:

1) A man must divorce his wife voluntarily;

2) He may only divorce his wife by means of a written document.

3) This document states that he is divorcing his wife and releasing her from his household.

4) The document completely severs the connection between the man and the woman.

5) The *get* is written specifically for the woman [to be divorced].

6) Once the *get* is written, there may be no other action necessary other than handing it to the woman.

7) The man hands the *get* to the woman, (she does not take it from him).

8) He hands it to her in the presence of witnesses.

9) He hands it to her for the purpose of divorcing her.

10) The husband or his agent must be the one who hands it to her.

The other requirements of a *get*, such as dating it, and having witnesses sign it, are Rabbinic ordinances.

THE SOURCE FOR DIVORCE IN THE TORAH

1:2. How do we know that these ten principles are Torah decrees? They are derived from the verse, "*If she is displeasing to him . . . he shall write her a bill of divorce and place it in her hand, and send her from his house*" (*Devarim* 24:1).

"*If she is displeasing to him*"—implies that he divorces her of his own free will. If a woman is divorced against her husband's will, the divorce is invalid. However, a woman may be divorced either voluntarily or against her will.[20]

1:3. "*He shall write*"—teaches that a woman can be divorced only through a written document;

"*for her*"—it should be written for her sake;

"*a bill of divorce*"—meaning, a document that severs the relationship between the man and woman without leaving him any control over her. If the bond between them is not entirely broken, the divorce is not effective, as will be explained.

1:4. "*He will place it in her hand*"—teaches that she is not divorced until the *get* is placed in her hand, in the hand of her agent—which is considered as her hand—or in her domain which is considered as her hand, as will be explained.

"*and send her from his house*"—the text of the *get* should indicate that he is sending her away, not sending himself away from her.

---

[20] This is the law as prescribed by the Talmud. However, the great Rabbeinu Gershom, *Meor Hagolah* (960-1040 C.E.) issued a ban against divorce without the wife's consent. This became law throughout Ashkenazic Jewry.

COMPELLING A RECALCITRANT HUSBAND
TO GIVE A GET

2:20. When a man is legally required to divorce his wife[21] but refuses to divorce her, the court beats him until he agrees, at which time a *get* is written, and considered valid. This applies everywhere and at all times, [not just in Eretz Yisrael or when the *Sanhedrin* existed].

Similarly, if Jews have non-Jews say [to the stubborn husband], "Do what the Jews tell you to do," beating him until he consents to divorce his wife, the *get* is satisfactory.

However, if the non-Jews, on their own accord, force him to write a *get*, the *get* is [Rabbinically] invalid. [It is valid by Torah law since this is a situation that] requires one to give a divorce.

Why isn't this *get* null and void? After all, he is being forced—either by Jews or non-Jews—to give the divorce against his will [and a *get* must be given willingly].

We consider a person to be coerced when he is compelled to do something the Torah does not require him to do, for example, if he was beaten until he agreed to a sale, or to give a present.

However, if a person's evil impulse drives him to avoid doing a mitzvah or to transgress, and he is beaten until he performs the mitzvah or refrains from doing the forbidden action, he is not considered as coerced. Rather, originally he was forced [to do the evil deed] by his own evil inclination.[22]

One who [seemingly] refuses to divorce his wife, really wants to be a good Jew, performing the mitzvos and keeping away from transgressions; however his evil impulse prods him [into refusing to

---

21   For example, a man whose wife says that she loathes him, or a man who was married to a woman for ten years without her bearing a child, or a man who is suffering from constant bad breath, or a *kohen* who marries a divorcee, all these men are required to divorce their wives (*Hilchos Ishus* 25:11-13).

22   The Rambam implies: In his heart, every Jew wants to observe the mitzvos; it is his *yetzer hara* that forces him to commit a sin. When he is beaten and compelled to renounce his evil ways and do the right thing, his innate goodness will emerge.

divorce her]. Therefore, when he is beaten until his evil impulse has been weakened, and he agrees [to divorce], he has given the *get* voluntarily.

If there are no legal grounds to require him to divorce, and a Jewish court or common people force him to give a *get*, this *get* is unsatisfactory. However, since Jews have coerced him, he is advised to go through with the divorce. On the other hand, if non-Jews force him to divorce when it was not legally required, the divorce is worthless.

Although he may have told non-Jews that he agreed, and told Jews to write and sign a *get*, since the law does not require him to give a *get*, and he was coerced by non-Jews to divorce, the *get* is null and void.

HILCHOS YIBBUM VECHALITZAH
LAWS OF YIBBUM AND CHALITZAH

WHAT IS YIBBUM AND CHALITZAH?[23]

1:1 It is a positive mitzvah of the Torah for a man to marry the widow of his paternal brother,[24] if his brother died without leaving children, as it says, "*If he died without leaving a son, her husband's brother shall come to her*" (*Devarim* 25:5). [This applies regardless whether she became a widow] after *nisuin* or after *erusin*.

Torah law does not require a man to consecrate his *yevamah* [through *kiddushin*] for she is his wife acquired for him by heaven; only intercourse is necessary. The money due to her for her *kesubah* (marriage contract) is paid from her late husband's estate.

1:2. If either the *yavam* or the *yevamah* does not want to perform *yibbum*, the *yavam* [releases her from this obligation through the ritual of] *chalitzah*. Afterwards she is free to marry another man.

---

[23] By Torah law, the widow of one who dies without children must marry her late husband's brother in a process called *yibum*. The widow is called a *yevamah* and her late husband's brother is referred to as a *yavam*. If the *yavam* refuses to perform *yibbum*, he must release the *yevamah* through the ritual of *chalitzah*, whereby the *yevamah* takes off the *yavam's* shoe and spits in front of him, after which she may marry another man.

[24] a brother to whom he is related through his father, but not a brother to whom he is related only through his mother.

It is a positive mitzvah of the Torah for the *yavam* to perform *chalitzah* if he does not want to perform *yibbum*, as it says, "*She shall take off his shoe . . .*" (*Devarim* 25:9).

The mitzvah of *yibbum* takes precedence over the mitzvah of *chalitzah*.[25]

1:3. The passage, "*If he died without leaving a son,*" [should not be taken literally]. [If the deceased brother] has any offspring be it a son, daughter, descendant of a son, or a descendant of a daughter—either from his widow or another woman his widow is free from the obligation of *chalitzah* or *yibbum*.

Even if he has a descendant who is illegitimate or an idol worshipper, the widow is free from the obligation of *chalitzah* or *yibbum*.

A CHILD BORN OF A NON-JEWISH WOMAN IS NOT JEWISH

1:4. [This applies if the children are born of a Jewish mother.] However, if [a deceased man] has a child born to a maidservant or a non-Jewish woman, his widow is not free of the obligation [of *yibbum* and *chalitzah*]. This is because the children of a maidservant are servants and the children of a non-Jewish woman are non-Jews, thus not related to him.

[This principle is derived from the following verses:] Concerning a maidservant it says, "*The woman and her children shall remain her master's property,*" (*Shemos* 21:4), implying that her children have the same status she has, [no matter who is the father]. And regarding a non-Jewish woman it says, "*They will lead your son away from Me*" (*Devarim* 7;4), meaning, [the non-Jewish mother] will prevent his being part of the Jewish community.

Even when a man's son born of a maidservant is freed, or his son

---

[25] Nowadays, *yibbum* is not performed, and *chalitzah* is universally carried out.

born of a non-Jewish woman converts, this does not cause his widow to be freed [from the obligation of *yibbum*, for, although the son converted or was freed, he is not considered related to the man who fathered him].

Even if one dies without fathering any children other than a child from a maidservant, then freed the son and mother and married her, his widow must perform *yibbum*, although the son [whom the deceased] fathered is alive and has been freed.

2:18. Before the *yavam* performs *yibbum* or *chalitzah* with the *yevamah*, she is forbidden to marry another man, for it says, "*The dead man's wife shall not be allowed to marry outside to a strange man*" (*Devarim* 25:5).

If she marries another person, and they have marital relations, both are punished with lashes, and he must divorce her with a *get*, even if she had several children with him. She is forbidden to him and to her *yavam*. Her *yavam* must perform *chalitzah* with her; then she may marry another man.

THE *CHALITZAH* RITUAL

4:1. How is the mitzvah of *chalitzah* performed?
The *yevamah* contacts the judges in the *yavam*'s town who then advise both of them. If *yibbum* is preferable, they counsel him to perform *yibbum*. Perhaps, she is a young girl and he is old and vice versa, in which case they advise him to perform *chalitzah*.

4:2. The judges first decide on a place to meet, and then the *yevamah* performs *chalitzah* in front of them, for it says, "*His yevamah shall go up to the elders in court*" (*Devarim* 5:7).

If [the judges] did not confer about the case not selecting a site, yet [the *yavam*] and [the *yevamah*] meet them and they perform the *chalitzah* on the spot, the *chalitzah* is valid.

4:6. How is *chalitzah* done? The *yavam* is given a leather shoe with a heel that is not sewn with linen threads. He places it on his right foot, tying its straps around his foot. The *yavam* and the *yevamah* stand before the *beis din* who read the phrase "*My* yavam *refuses*" (*Devarim* 25:7) in Hebrew for the *yevamah* to repeat. Afterwards, they read the phrase, "*I do not want to take her*" (*Devarim* 25:8) for the *yavam* to repeat.

Then the *yavam* pushes his foot against the floor. The *yevamah* sits on the floor, extends her hand before the *beis din,* loosens the straps of his shoe, removes it, and throws it on the floor. As soon as she removes the majority [of the shoe from his foot], she is free to marry another man.

4:7. Then she stands and spits on the floor in front of his face, so the saliva can be seen by the judges. The mitzvah of *chalitzah* requires the *yevamah* and *yavam* stand when they recite [the phrases] and when she spits. Furthermore, the judges must see the saliva coming out of her mouth.

Finally the [Beis Din] recites "*This is what shall be done to the man who will not build up a family for his brother. The name of that place shall then be known in Yisrael as, 'The house where the shoe was removed.*" (*Devarim* 25:9,10).

HILCHOS ISSUREI BIAH

LAWS CONCERNING FORBIDDEN RELATIONS

━━━◉━━━

LAWS OF CONVERSION

13:1. The Jews entered the covenant [with Hashem] through three acts: circumcision, immersion, and the offering of sacrifices.

13:2. Circumcision—took place in Egypt [before the offering of the *korban Pesach*] as it says, "*No uncircumcised man may eat [the sacrifice]* (*Shemos* 12:48). Moshe Rabbeinu circumcised the people, who—excepting the tribe of Levi—had stopped performing *bris milah* in Egypt. [In praise of the tribe of Levi,] it says, "*They safeguarded Your covenant*" (*Devarim* 33:9).

13:3. Immersion—was performed in the wilderness before the Giving of the Torah, as it says, "*Sanctify them today and tomorrow. Let them [even] immerse their clothing*" (*Shemos* 19:10).

Sacrifices—were also brought then, as it says, "*He sent the youths of the children of Yisrael and they offered burnt offerings*" (*Shemos* 24:5). These sacrifices were offered on behalf of the entire Jewish people.

13:4. This process has remained in force for all future generation. When a non-Jew wishes to enter into the covenant, sheltering under the wings of the *Shechinah*, and accepting the yoke of Torah, he undergoes circumcision, immerses, and offers a sacrifice. A woman who converts must also immerse and offer a sacrifice. For it says, "*You and the convert shall be alike*" (*Bamidbar* 15:15), meaning: Just as you entered the covenant with circumcision, immersion, and the offering of a sacrifice, so too, in future generations, a convert must undergo circumcision, immersion, and bring a sacrifice.

13:5. What sacrifice must a convert bring? One animal as a burnt offering or two turtledoves or pigeons, both being brought as burnt offerings. Today since we do not offer sacrifices, a convert requires circumcision and immersion; bringing his sacrifice when the *Beis Hamikdash* is rebuilt.

13:6. One is not considered a convert until he both circumcises and immerses. Circumcision without immersion or vice versa is not enough.

He must immerse in the presence of three men [who constitute a *beis din*]. Since a *beis din* is required, he may not immerse on Shabbos, Yom Tov, or during the night, [since a *beis din* does not convene at those times]. However, if he did immerse at those times, he is a convert nonetheless.

The Conversion

14:1. By which procedure is a righteous convert accepted? When a non-Jew wishes to convert, and after investigating his background, we find no ulterior motive, we ask him, "What prompted you to convert? Don't you know that presently the Jews are tormented, oppressed, harassed, and made to suffer?" If he answers, "I am aware of this yet I only wish to be worthy to be one of them," we accept him immediately.

14:2. We then inform him of the fundamental principles of our faith, namely, the oneness of God and the prohibition against worshipping false gods, elaborating in great detail about this. We also mention some mitzvos, both easier and more serious, but we do not detail them. We familiarize him with the laws of *leket, shik'chah, pei'ah,*[26] and tithing and the punishment for neglecting them.

We also tell him about the punishment for violating the mitzvos, saying "Before you convert, you are not punished by *kareis*[27] for eating forbidden fats, you are not punished by stoning for desecrating the Shabbos. But after you convert, if you eat forbidden fats, you are liable to *kareis*. If you desecrate the Shabbos, you are liable to being stoned to death."

We do not teach every detail which might upset him, causing him to recant. Initially, we invite a [prospective convert] with gentle and pleasing words, as it says, "*I drew them with human ties, with cords of love*" (*Hoshea* 11:4).

14:3. Just as we tell him the punishment [for violating] the mitzvos, we describe the reward for fulfilling them. We explain that by observing the mitzvos he earns everlasting life in the World to Come, and that one can only be perfectly righteous, if he acquires wisdom observing and knowing all the mitzvos.

14:4. We tell him: Know that the World to Come is set aside for the righteous, namely, the Jewish people. The misery Jews suffer in this world is a blessing in disguise. Were they to receive an abundance of good things as do the non-Jews, they might become arrogant going astray and losing their reward in the World to Come, as it says, "*Yeshurun became fat and rebelled*" (*Devarim* 32:15).

14:5. [We tell the prospective convert:] The Holy One, blessed be He, causes [the Jewish people] to suffer severely so they should not perish; the other nations will perish, and the Jewish people will sur-

---

26 *Leket* — Not to pick up individual stalks that have fallen, but leave them in the field for the poor.

  Shich'chah — not to turn back to pick up a forgotten sheaf.

  Pei'ah — not to harvest the ends of the field

27 excision of the soul, premature death.

vive triumphantly. We speak at length about this, showing our love. If he decides not to accept the mitzvos, he goes on his way. But if he accepts the mitzvos, we circumcise him immediately. If he was already circumcised, we [make a small incision on his male organ,] drawing a drop of "blood of *bris*." We wait until recovers completely, then he immerses.

IMMORAL BEHAVIOR

21:1. When a person is intimate with one of the *arayos*[28] without performing the sexual act, or, if driven by lust, he embraces and kisses her, taking pleasure in physical contact, he receives lashes as prescribed by the Torah. For it says, *"Do not follow any of the perverted practices that were done before you"* (*Vayikra* 18:30). Furthermore it says, *"A man shall not approach a close relative to uncover her nakedness"* (*Vayikra* 18:6), meaning: We are forbidden to take preliminary steps which lead to sexual relations.

21:2. A person who does any of the above mentioned things, is suspect to engage in forbidden sexual relations.

One is forbidden to gesture with his hands or feet, wink at, banter with or act playfully with one of the *arayos*. It is forbidden to smell her perfume, or gaze at her beauty. One who intentionally acts this way receives lashes for rebellious conduct.

Gazing even at the small finger of a woman for pleasure is considered looking at her private parts. It is forbidden to listen to the [singing] voice of a woman or to gaze at her hair.

21:3. It is also forbidden to engage in these actions with women with whom relations are forbidden merely by a negative commandment.[29]

---

[28] The term *arayos* refers to incestuous unions between blood relations: a man and his mother, sister, daughter, grand-daughter . . . the wife of blood relations, and the wife's blood-relations, as set forth in *Vayikra*, chapter 18.

[29] Violation of a negative commandment is punishable by lashes, whereas *arayos*, incest, is punishable by *kareis* (*Vayikra* 18:29).

One may look intently at the face of an unmarried women—whether she is a virgin or no longer so—deciding if she is attractive so he may marry her. There is no prohibition against this, in fact this is proper.[30] However, he should not look at her in a sensual way. Indeed, it says, "*I made a covenant with my eyes not to gaze at a maiden*" (*Iyov* 31:1).

21:4. A man may gaze at his wife when she is menstrually unclean, though she is forbidden to him at that time. Although looking at her gives him pleasure, he will not have relations with her, since he knows she will be permitted to him later on. However, he may not engage in levity or act frivolously with her, since this may lead to sin.

21:5. Any woman—whether adult or minor, servant or free—may not do personal tasks for a man, to avoid lustful thoughts. This includes washing his face, hands or feet, making his bed in his presence, or pouring him a cup [of wine]. These tasks are performed for a man only by his wife. A man should not greet a woman or inquire about her welfare at all, even through a messenger.

21:6. When a person embraces or kisses a woman forbidden to him as *arayos* such as his adult sister, or his mother's sister, or the like, though he is disinterested in and not aroused by her, he is doing an indecent thing. This is forbidden, and he is acting foolishly. One does not show affection to a woman forbidden to him as an *ervah*,[31] whether she is an adult or a minor, except a mother to her son and a father to his daughter.

21:32. A person should not marry the daughter of an *am haaretz*

---

[30] The Gemara in *Kiddushin* 41a says: A man may not consecrate a woman before he has seen her, for later he may find her repulsive, and she becomes loathsome to him.

[31] An *ervah* is a woman forbidden because of an incestuous union.

(unlearned person). For if he dies or is exiled,[32] his children will grow up to be unlearned, since their mother has no knowledge of the beauty of Torah.[33] Nor should he marry his daughter to an *am haaretz*. This is like tying her and placing her before a lion. [The *am haaretz* husband] may strike her and have marital relations with her without shame.

One should sell everything he owns to marry the daughter of a Torah scholar. For if he dies or is exiled, his children will grow up to be Torah scholars. And one should marry his daughter to a Torah scholar, for there is no shameful conduct or discord in the home of a Torah scholar.

PROHIBITION AGAINST BEING ALONE WITH A WOMAN

22:1. It is forbidden to be alone with a woman forbidden as *arayos*, whether she is elderly or young, for this leads to intimacy. The only exceptions are a woman and her son, a father and his daughter, and a husband with his wife who is in her menstrual period.

If one's bride menstruates before he had marital relations with her, he is forbidden to be alone with her, [since they may not be able to control their sexual urge]. Rather, she sleeps among other women, and he sleeps among other men. If they had relations once, before she became menstrually unclean, he is allowed to be alone with her.

22:2. Jewish men are above suspicion of engaging in sexual relations with men or with animals. Therefore, there is no prohibition against being alone [with a man or an animal]. Nevertheless, if a person avoids being alone even with a man or an animal, it is com-

---

[32] A person who unintentionally murders someone, is exiled to one of the cities of refuge where he is safe from the avenger. He has to stay there until the death of the *Kohen Gadol* (*Bamidbar* 35:9-30).

[33] We assume that after her husband's death, the wife will return to her unlearned father's house where her children will grow up without a Torah education.

mendable. Famous sages stayed away from animals never being alone with them.

The prohibition against being alone with a woman forbidden as *arayos* has been transmitted by the Oral Torah.

22:3. After the episode of Amnon and Tamar,[34] David and his *beis din* issued a decree prohibiting a man to be alone with an unmarried woman. Although an unmarried woman is not an *ervah*, being alone with her is considered being alone in the company of an *ervah*. Shammai and Hillel issued a prohibition against being alone with a non-Jewess.

Consequently, if someone secludes himself with a woman—whether Jewish or non-Jewish—with whom he is forbidden to be alone, both the man and woman are given lashes for rebellious behavior, and their impropriety is publicized. An exception is made when a man is alone with a married woman, although it is forbidden, no lashes are given if he secludes himself with her, to prevent rumors from spreading that she committed adultery, thus casting aspersions that her children are *mamzerim*.[35]

22:4. If a man's wife is nearby, he may be alone with another woman, because his wife guards him [against immorality]. However, a Jewish woman should not seclude herself with a non-Jewish man, even if his wife is around. For a non-Jew's wife will not guard her husband [against wrongdoing], and a non-Jew has no shame, [and may have relations with her while his wife is around].

22:17. The secrets[36] of forbidden sexual relations may not be expounded to three students. While one student will question the

---

[34] In 2 Shmuel, chapter 13, we read that Amnon, David's oldest son, became infatuated with his half-sister, Tamar. He pretended to be sick and asked Tamar to serve him a light meal. When she came to serve him the meal, he ordered everyone to leave. He then overpowered and raped her.

[35] offspring from a forbidden union

[36] According to Rashi, such forbidden relations are not explicitly mentioned in the Torah, but are inferred.

teacher, the other two may argue about the subject matter, not attending the teacher. Since people are drawn to forbidden relations, if one is in doubt about something he heard, he will [mistakenly] rule leniently. Therefore, we only teach two students, so that each one will concentrate and remember what he heard from the teacher.

22:18. There is nothing more difficult for most people to avoid than sexual wrongdoing and forbidden intercourse. Our Sages explained: When the Jews were commanded regarding forbidden sexual relations they cried and accepted this mitzvah with resentment and weeping, as it says, "*Moshe heard the people weeping with their families*" (*Bamidbar* 11:10), meaning, they cried because of family matters [i.e., regarding incest which was now forbidden to them].

22:19. Our Sages said: Man has an innate craving for robbery and forbidden sexual relations. In every community there are people who are promiscuous about forbidden sexual relationships and prohibited marital intercourse. In the same vein, our Sages said: Most people are guilty of robbery,[37] a minority are guilty of forbidden sexual relations, and everyone is guilty of a slight suggestion of slander.[38]

22:20. Therefore, one should subdue his deep-seated impulses training himself in extra holiness, pure thought, and proper character traits to be shielded against them.

He should avoid being alone with a woman, for this leads [to transgression]. Our Sages used to tell their students, "Guard me from [sinning with] my daughter;" "Guard me from [sinning with] my daughter-in-law." They meant to teach their students not to be

---

[37] In business, people tend to commit robbery by being careless about overcharging or not paying the full price of labor (*Rashi*).

[38] Not actual, but implied slander. For example, to say, "There is fire in the oven of So-and-so," suggesting that they are wealthy and eating all the time.

embarrassed about such things and avoid being alone with a woman.

22:21. By the same token, a person should stay away from hilarity, drunkenness, and flirtation. These things open the door and lead to forbidden relations. A man should not live without a wife. [for being married] brings about great purity.

The Sages said: Directing all one's thoughts toward the teachings of the Torah and gaining a thorough understanding of wisdom is the most effective way to purify one's thoughts. For thoughts of forbidden relations take only gain a foothold in a mind empty of wisdom.[39] Describing the beauty of wisdom, Shlomoh says, "*A loving doe, a graceful mountain goat. Let her breasts satisfy you at all times. Be infatuated with love of her always*" (*Mishlei* 5:19).

---

[39] *Kiddushin* 30b

GLOSSARY

ADAR - The twelfth Hebrew month
BEIS DIN - Jewish court
BEIS HAMIKDASH - Holy Temple
BERACHAH pl. *BERACHOS*: - blessing
CHALITZAH - the ceremony whereby a woman whose husband left no progeny is released
CHASAN - groom
CHAZZAN - leader of the prayer service
EIRUSIN - betrothal
ERVAH - one forbidden because of an incestuous union
GALUS - exile
GEMARA - Talmud
HAFTARA - a portion of the Prophets that is read publicly on Shabbos and holidays
HALACHAH - law
HASHEM - God
KALLAH - bride
KESUVAH - marriage contract
KIDDUSH - a declaration sanctifying the beginning of a holy day
KOHEIN pl. *KOHANIM* - Priests, descendants of Aaron
MASHIACH - The Messiah
MESADER KIDDUSHIN - one who officiates at a marriage
MILAH - circumcision
MINHAG pl. *MINHAGIM* - customs
MISHNAH - compilation of the oral tradition; it also refers to one paragraph of this compilation.
MITZVAH pl. *MITZVOS* - commandment
ROSH CHODESH - the first day of the Hebrew month
SEFER - book or scroll
SHABBOS - The day of rest - Saturday
SHACHARIS - the morning prayer
SHECHINA - Divine Presence
SHEMONEH ESREI - the eighteen-beracha prayer that we say thrice each day
SUKKOS - Festival of Tabernacles
TEFILLIN - phylacteries
TEHILLIM - Psalms
TESHUVA - repentance
YAMIM TOVIM - holidays
YETZER HARA - evil inclination
YIBBUM - levirate marriage